RENOVATING FOR PROFIT

CHERIE BARBER

RENOVATING FOR PROFIT

CHERIE BARBER

hardie grant books

CONTENTS

INTRODUCTION

Fairy tales are for princesses

The first thing you need to know about me is that my story isn't a Cinderella story. There's no overnight success in what I've achieved – it's been a long hard slog. And there are plenty of mistakes I've made along the way. So. Many. Mistakes.

This is a story about working things out the hard way, making sacrifices, taking risks, following your instincts and remaining true to yourself.

Doing all that got me to where I am today ... and where is that? I have personally completed more than 100 renovations and hold an impressive property portfolio, which means I could retire at any time – but I don't plan to. I love what I do. I own Australia's leading renovation education company, Renovating For Profit, with Australia's largest community of renovators, and I run sold-out masterclasses across the country. Along the way, the media dubbed me Australia's Renovation Queen and the name has stuck ever since. I've been on all the major Australian TV networks and my skills have seen me renovate homes in Australia, Asia and the USA. Each week, I take to the radio airwaves to talk about my favourite topic: renovating! There are awards and lots of other things, but I won't bore you with those details.

But one thing is for sure: life hasn't always been like this.

Family matters

I was born in 1970, to your average working-class family. I am the oldest of seven kids (including step siblings) and was raised in Penrith in Sydney's western suburbs. Yes, I'm officially a Westie. Growing up, money was always in short supply. There were hand-me-downs, caravan-park holidays, shared bedrooms and all that. Best time of my life.

My adorable dad is the hardest worker I know. He was an earthmover, working seven days a week in an effort to keep us all fed. Some of my earliest memories are sitting on the side of his tractor, as a three-year-old, watching him manoeuvre around a building site, cutting into and levelling out the ground for new home sites. Maybe that's where it all started?

I was 15 years old when Mum and Dad got divorced. Up until that point, my mother had been the stay-at-home mum, raising us kids while Dad worked hard to keep the bills paid. Suddenly single and in need of money, Mum applied for job after job, but was never given a chance. Who was going to employ her with no qualifications or employment history? Her will was there, but the rejections came in thick and fast.

Left: Me, aged one. This will be the only time in my life that I have a mohawk.

Right: My sister and I on the back of my dad's earthmoving truck. And yes, I'm the one with the Harry High-Pants.

After taking more knockbacks than Muhammad Ali, Mum decided to take matters into her own hands. Don't ask me how, but she managed to get a personal loan for $30,000. She bought her own business – a weird little haberdashery store that also sold old lady dresses. From the start, it was never going to succeed. She added instant scratchies, lotto and videos to make it even more bizarre, but at least those three additions kept the business afloat. But there was no profit. She had dug herself deeper into a financial grave.

With not enough money, Mum found herself back in the same situation, applying for jobs. She eventually got a nurse's aide job, emptying bedpans and the like. She tried to sell the business – to pay off the personal loan – but nobody wanted it. So she hauled me out of school, at the start of Year 11, to run the shop while she worked elsewhere.

I worked in that shop for two years, from the age of 16 to 18. I got paid sixty bucks. I'd wake up at the crack of dawn, travel two hours to get there for opening time at eight, I'd sit in the empty store all day long, then close it at six and make the long commute home again. There certainly weren't any tears from me when she finally sold that shop! I re-enrolled in school, but lasted only 6 weeks. I had matured beyond my years and found it very difficult to re-adjust to a classroom environment.

I got a full-time job working as an assistant video store manager, which I played out for a year. I then moved to 3M, a large global company that had 40,000 different products at the time. I would spend the next nine years of my life there, rising through the ranks of various marketing positions. It's where I learnt strategy, systems, processes and business management; skills that would later become a big part of my success.

It was 1990, I had a serious job and was on $36,000 per annum. My boyfriend worked at the same company and together, we saved like crazy.

The accidental renovator

In 1991, at age 21, I bought my first property with my partner. We went halves on a $212,000 vinyl-clad house on a main road in Sydney. Actually, on a six-lane major arterial road – what were we thinking?

Obviously, this was a great lesson on the consequences of not doing your real estate due diligence. As soon as we moved in, we realised the terrible mistake we'd made. We couldn't sleep – every night, all night. The noise from trucks screaming past would constantly wake us up. At the time, the house had been the only property we could afford to buy. And we didn't know what we were doing.

We made the decision to sell and get out. We'd only just moved in! But first we had to make some changes, so as not to lose money. With zero funds in the bank to hire tradespeople, our DIY journey began.

The house had heritage green and fuchsia walls, so we painted over those, in plain old white. I ripped up the grungy old carpet and exposed the timber floors. We had no money to polish them so we left them in their original condition. Then we went on a rampage with garden clippers and a lawnmower, getting the unruly front and backyard in pristine order.

We put the house back on the market and made a small profit. That was my first taste at making money, a different way, outside of a normal job. I had just become an accidental renovator.

We bought our next property straight after, on a much quieter street, for $270,000. It was a cosmetically tired two-storey house, with a bit of structural work required at the rear. I got a second job at a Leagues Club, picking up dirty glasses, emptying bins, handing out prawns on function nights, and everything in between.

I would spend the next eight years renovating the house, while holding down two jobs. My day job paid for my half of the mortgage and my night job paid for the reno. When I wasn't working, I was renovating our house, slowly, inch by inch. On Saturday nights, I wasn't out nightclubbing – I was at home painting!

In 1999, my boyfriend and I split. To this day we remain great mates, but, interestingly, he never renovated again. We sold the house for $863,000 and after all debts were paid out, we split the proceeds in two. I now had $175,000 in net wealth, aged 29.

Top: Steve and I in one of our very first press features.

Bottom left: One of my early structural renovations.
I look hardcore!

Bottom right: A family photo with our daughter, Milan,
aged three. Is she going to be a renovator? No, she's going to be a fashion designer. All the trips to the hardware
store have turned her off renovating for life!

Finding my place

Around the same time, I landed a new marketing role for a global cosmetics company. I was surrounded by luxury goods, wore pretty dresses and stilettos to work every day and got free perfume and cosmetics, but I wasn't in love with this scene. I was a slave to my corporate job – long hours, stress, work on the weekends. I was officially stuck in the pinstripe jail.

One day, a rather handsome chap flew by me on his motorcycle when I was driving my car. He turned back and we caught each other's eye. His name was Steve and, by the end of our very first date, it was love. We would spend the next 12 years of our lives together. You can imagine my joy when I learned he was just as passionate about property as me. Jackpot!

Renovations had gotten under my skin (in a good way) and while Steve had no experience in that department, he was keen to embrace it. We threw ourselves into the market and did three months intensive due diligence. I studied the market intensely, looked at what properties were selling for and attended open houses and auctions galore. Agents asked why we were going through every single open house on our weekends. Over time, I developed my own system and process to analyse property prices.

After three months of intensive research, we picked up a little 3-bedroom gem for $537,000. We were both working full-time still, in our normal jobs, but managed to complete the cosmetic renovation in just eight weeks. We had the tradespeople coming and going during the day. We visited the house every second night, after work, to make sure the tradespeople were doing what they were supposed to be doing. Not all of them did. We had some bumps along the way, but nothing catastrophic.

All up, we spent $150,000 in total project costs (including stamp duty, reno and resale costs). As soon as the reno was complete, it went to auction. We held an auction party on a Friday night with music, waiters, canapés. There was a thunderstorm with torrential rain, yet 150 people rocked up to witness the action. The hammer went down at $955,000, setting a new suburb record in the process. I almost wet my pants with excitement.

I quit my full-time job a few weeks later and threw myself into renovating. I was now a professional renovator, or so I thought.

Lessons learned

And so my new life had well and truly begun. I swapped my stilettos for steelcaps and was on top of the world and super happy to be my own boss. We re-invested every cent of profit into our next project and in that first year alone we bought six unrenovated properties with a combined value of $6.5 million, most of this done with other people's money. There was nothing stopping us – a formidable duo, you could say. We started to get noticed at local property auctions by the press as 'that reno couple'.

We went on to renovate a lot of properties together over the next decade. I was on-site each day, project managing, while Steve kept working for others for the first few years. He took jobs in finance, to learn the ins and outs of the industry.

I'm the queen of spray guns too!

New for old: DIY expert Cherie Barber teaches people the secrets to renovating their homes, like this one she is renewing in Annandale   Picture: Justin Lloyd

Watching paint dry can be fun — and profitable

THE moment the auction hammer went down to sell Cherie Barber's first renovated property she knew it was time to leave her job in marketing.

She had caught the renovating bug. "I was doing dances on the inside when the auction was over and that day was the catalyst for me," Ms Barber says.

"I threw in my job and went on to do six projects in my first year for a $115 million profit," she says.

Ms Barber has taught more than 2200 people in her Renovate for Profit courses over the past two years, which has earned her the title of Australia's "renovation queen".

Ms Barber might be an expert at

buying, renovating and selling for profit but her No. 1 tip for improving your home is a simple coat of paint.

"Painting is quick, cheap and offers a high impact," she says.

This week *The Daily Telegraph* is offering readers a series of mini-books brimming with simple tips on renovating inside and out. The eight-part

series started last Sunday and continues today with *Better Backyard*, a guide to improving the outside of your home.

Tomorrow's mini-book is *Paint Essentials*. The books cost $2 each with your newspaper.

Today's coupon: page 87

One of my early press clippings as a renovation powerhouse.

There has been so much blood, sweat and tears along the way. I only know what I know now because I've made mistakes. I'm the first to admit I've made every single conceivable mistake that could possibly be made in renovating. I've been ripped off by tradespeople, installed things in the wrong order, shopped in the wrong places for fixtures and fittings, been in trouble with the local council, and found myself in court even! All through lack of knowledge. The reality is, there was no-one around to mentor us. We had to learn the hard way. Nothing beats brutal life experience, especially in the renovation game.

This book is all about what I know because of those errors. To get you thinking, I've made a list of my top five mistakes.

TOP 5 MISTAKES

1. Getting ripped off by tradespeople

Now I know: GET QUOTES. Always get three quotes so you can benchmark
a price when you don't know the true value of something.

2. Being disorganised

You need to sit down and plan out your reno.
Winging it won't be good for your bank balance.

3. Paying too much for stuff and not knowing where to shop

You have to do your research because you can always
get things for a better price if you shop around.

4. Not knowing how to solve disputes with tradespeople

Sometimes you need to back yourself and stand your ground,
even if you're tiny in stature, like me!

5. No end goal in sight

If you're renovating to sell or rent, you need to keep that in your mind's
eye throughout the project. Start with the end in mind!

Renovating can be full of heartbreak and back break, but there's so much satisfaction to be gained too. I am self-taught, I don't give up and I feel proud of what I've created as a result of my hard work. And you can do it too. But like I said, don't lose sight of that end goal.

After almost two decades of renovating professionally, I've developed processes and systems that enable me to do my renovations in a cookie-cutter fashion for time, cost and process efficiencies. I no longer make all those mistakes I used to make.

People always seemed fascinated by what we did, often drilling us with questions – how do you do this? How do you do that? This curiosity led to the next step in my renovating journey.

Renovating For Profit

In 2009 we opened Renovating For Profit, a company designed to teach people a structured process for how we did what we did, day in and day out. And from the moment the company opened, it took off like wildfire. Instant success. To this very day, eight years later, I have sold-out masterclasses and talks around the country.

Unfortunately, Steve and I split in 2012, but to this day he is one of my best friends and we have a beautiful daughter, who is the apple of our eyes. Yes, among all that craziness, I managed to have a baby! But since we separated, Steve also quit renovating! See a pattern there?

I've continued my renovation journey solo ever since, proving that you can renovate by yourself. While two heads are always helpful, it's not essential in renovating. Just back yourself with a good system and a wheelbarrow full of passion and enthusiasm.

Moreover, in the last six years, the media noticed my renovation prowess. I scored TV gigs for Foxtel, networks 7 and 9 and I am a regular TV renovator for Network Ten's *The Living Room*. I've been on this show from its inception six years ago, and it's fun! In 2015, I gained international attention, landing my own TV show in the USA called *5 Day Flip*. In 2016, I jumped on a plane to do a guest role for *The Apartment*, one of the biggest renovation shows in Asia. I've written renovation columns galore for magazines and done hundreds of interviews on the topic of renovation. It keeps me busy. Not bad for a girl from out west, who never finished high school.

The long and short of it is this: I've worked bloody hard over the last 27 years. Renovation isn't for the faint of heart, but if you've got the determination, your efforts will be financially rewarded. It's not a hard process but it does require effort. It's not a free road to wealth so be prepared to work.

Everyone buys property at different life stages, and sometimes you have to take five steps backwards to move ten steps forward. I worked a second job, I made sacrifices, but that's what's required to get ahead in life and work. If you don't have the deposit to buy a property, you'll need to get one together. Put luxuries on hold, sell stuff you don't need, get a second job, go without. That's what you have to do.

Before you start, I've summed up the key things you'll need to have at the ready for your renovation.

My American trade crew on *5 Day Flip*. Just missing one crew member, Jerry.
The nicest bunch of blokes anyone could wish for on a reno site.

KEY THINGS YOU NEED

1. An unrenovated property

When you buy a place to renovate, you need to do your due diligence, which means you need to study the market and buy a property that genuinely has good potential for the value of the property to be increased. Where and what type of property you buy makes all the difference.

2. A solid plan of attack

You know the saying, 'Failing to plan is planning to fail'. Enough said.

3. A black book of great tradespeople

Knowing who to ask for help is going to make your life so much easier. Communicating clearly with tradespeople is KEY.

And you know what else? An inexperienced renovator can fall at the last hurdle, when you put your property up for sale or auction. This is what I mean about keeping the end game in sight.

Once you finish your reno, don't just hand everything over to your real estate agent and hope for the best.

Maintain control, right to the very end. Have weekly meetings, ask how many buyers have shown interest and what the feedback is. A good agent remains accountable.

And just like a theatre production, your open house needs attention to detail to set the scene.

CHERIE'S GOLDEN RULES FOR AN OPEN HOUSE

1. Always get your property professionally styled.

2. See the light! Turn on all lights, open the blinds and have lemon citrus scents filtering through your home.

3. Tidy up the garden beds and make the front look appealing.

4. Sweep pathways and your back deck. No leaves anywhere!

5. Create a nice mood and setting with candles and soft furnishings.

6. Remove all personal photos – you need to create a neutral setting that your buyers or renters can see themselves in.

7. Touches like fresh flowers and potted plants really lift your space.

8. Always get your house set up and ready for an open house yourself. Never leave this responsibility to your real estate agent.

9. Produce a fact sheet on the property highlighting all its features. Make everything super obvious, so buyers see all the good stuff at a glance. I have little templates for this very thing (see opposite).

10. Have a building and pest inspection already done and leave copies of those reports on your kitchen bench, ready to hand out. It helps your buyers make a quick decision. Strike while the iron is hot!

KITCHEN	KEY INCLUSIONS
	• New kitchen doors & end panels. • New benchtops. • New kitchen appliances. • New flooring. • Freshly painted walls, ceilings & trims. • New lighting. • High-end fixtures & fittings.

I have a million templates (slight exaggeration). This is one type that I stick on the wall in every room when I am selling a property. Don't rely on your real estate agent to communicate every feature to your buyers!

But maybe I'm jumping the gun here. You have to get started first ...

This book goes through each of the main rooms in a home and details the best tricks and tips to help your house shine, without breaking the bank. It seems as though everyone is renovating on a budget these days. Who has $50,000 to spend on a kitchen? From the lounge room to the bedroom, you'll be reading about my favourite renovation ideas and traps to avoid – I certainly know when to spend and when to save – and about a few of my secret budgeting tricks too. I wish I had this book when I first started!

I'm so proud of what all my students are achieving right now. I look forward to hearing about the success of your very own project. Drop me a line on www.facebook.com/renoforprofit.

Happy renovating! With much love,

CHAPTER ONE

FANCY FACADES

We've all heard it before: 'First impressions count'. But in the real estate game, do they really?

Like it or not, in the same way that people judge other people by their appearance, they will judge the place you live in. Some would say that you can tell a lot about a home owner by the appearance of their house.

A shabby-looking exterior is likely to deter potential buyers – and will most likely annoy your neighbours. On the flipside, a well-presented home will grab people's attention from the very first second they lay eyes on it. And you want it to be **love at first sight** for the home owner to be.

STREET APPEAL

How far should you go in making your facade look great? Let's not kid ourselves, at street level, many places are full of ugly houses. But there is no valid reason to ever leave them like that. Every day, I tackle the downright ugly with great gusto and love it! Creating great street appeal is easier than you think, and with a little bit of insider knowledge, you can go from drabulous to fabulous in next to no time. But before I reveal some easy ways to do that, let's cover some of my essential rules for creating great street appeal, sooner rather than later.

GOLDEN RULE #1

As a general rule of thumb,
spend no more than 1.5% of your property value transforming the facade of your house.
For example, if your property is currently valued at $600,000, you should spend no more than $9000 on a fully finished facade reno – not a single cent more. Anything over this and you risk becoming another shudder-inducing statistic of someone who spent too much and never saw a return on their investment.

GOLDEN RULE #2

It's never good to have multiple personalities, and your front facade is no exception. I've seen more bad alterations and additions than you can poke a stick at. It gives new meaning to what the … ? Beautiful little character cottages ruined with sleek horizontal slat fences (instead of cute little picket ones), faux plastic fretwork on 1970s red brick homes (aarrgghh!), modern decks on the front of quaint Californian bungalows (wrong!) – I've seen my fair share of shockers that could have been totally avoided.

When it comes to your facade, you've got to be strategic. That means one theme, not two. Your house should be either traditional or modern, there's no in between. Be aware of the different architectural styles and where your property fits into that mix. Respect the age and character of your home, or the lack of it. Even drab 1970s and 1980s red, brown or blonde brick houses or those famed fibro-clad houses can be instantly modernised, even though they had little character to begin with.

With the above in mind, let's go through my top facade changes. You'll be glad to know that none of them are hard or complicated.

ARCHITECTURAL STYLES

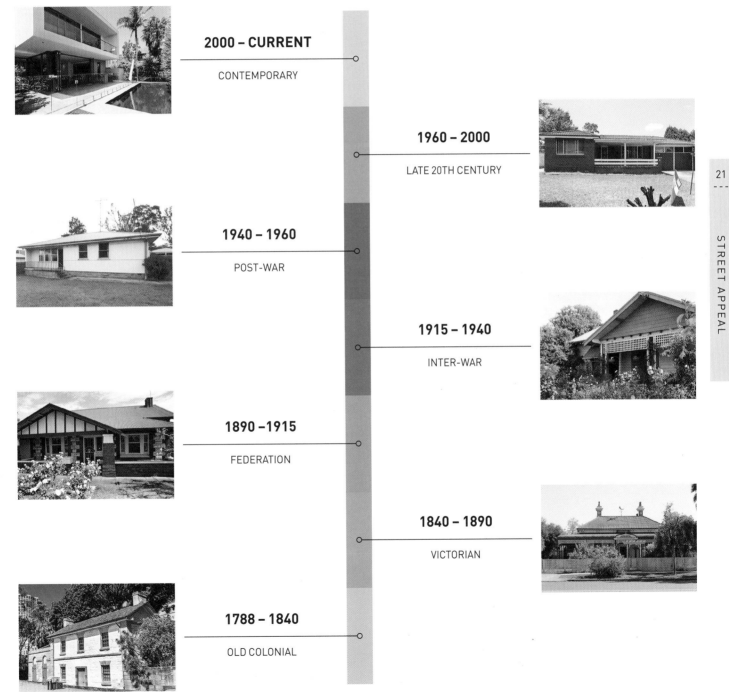

2000 – CURRENT

CONTEMPORARY

1960 – 2000

LATE 20TH CENTURY

1940 – 1960

POST-WAR

1915 – 1940

INTER-WAR

1890 –1915

FEDERATION

1840 – 1890

VICTORIAN

1788 – 1840

OLD COLONIAL

RITZY ROOFS

It all starts with your roof. It's one of the largest visual masses on your facade, and hideous roof tiles are in plentiful supply around the nation. You'll find roof tiles covered in dirt, grime and dust, overgrown with a frenzy of moss, and discoloured and faded from years of battering from sun, wind and rain.

As a property owner, avoid roof replacement at all costs. You'll easily drop somewhere between $15,000 and $30,000 for an average roof to be replaced, yet it adds no value according to the bank. Don't replace – refresh your old roof tiles instead.

Your first port of call is to get your roof professionally cleaned. Depending on the company you use, expect to shell out somewhere between $750 and $1500 for a professional high-pressure-water clean. This is definitely not one of those tasks you want to do yourself, always leave this to the professionals. I've heard too many stories of young and perfectly fit individuals who've attempted the task, fallen off their roofs and never been the same again. Don't worry, there will be plenty of other DIY jobs you can do.

So in come the professionals (just google roof sprayers and you'll be on your way). Within a few hours, they'll blast the hell out of your roof tiles and a whole lot of dirty residue run-off will happen as a result. Once your roof dries, stand back and gaze lovingly at how much better it looks than it did just a few hours earlier.

But sometimes even a roof clean just won't cut the mustard due to discolouration. And this is where the magic of roof spraying comes in. Again, prices vary according to which roof sprayer does the job, but presto, within three days, your roof will look brand-new. In fact, people will think you've replaced your roof completely when really you haven't. Roof spraying typically costs between $2500 and $5000 but is well worth it, especially if you are giving your facade a new lick of paint where the roof no longer suits your new colour scheme.

HOT TIP

When renovating your facade, always start with the highest area first (your roof), then work all the way down to ground level, with your landscaping the last piece of work to be done.

Over the course of three days, professional roof sprayers start with a high-pressure clean, removing all grime that's been anchored to your tiles for years. The next step is repointing and fixing all your broken tiles. Once that's done, they'll spray one coat of primer, which helps your paint bond to your tiles. The last steps of the process are two coats of good-quality external paint.

I have to admit there is one renovation that still haunts me to this day. It was one of my early TV renovations and the home owners' budget was so tight that roof spraying wasn't an option. We could only afford a roof clean. We renovated everything in this house, internally and externally, except the roof. When the project was done and dusted, guess what stood out like dogs' balls? Yup, the roof (check out the following pages to see what I mean).

I'm a big lover of roof spraying but I have to warn you, this is one area where a lot of cowboys exist. Prices can vary greatly between tradespeople depending on whether you want a quality job or a dodgy one. Some workers refuse to wear a safety harness even though laws exist around this – most roof sprayers must wear one. You also have your fair share of tradespeople with no insurance (even though they tell you they have it), so always sight their insurance papers in person to minimise the risk of being sued if an accident occurs.

FANCY FACADES

BEFORE

This late 20th century house wasn't doing anyone (or the street) any favours! It had ugly red bricks, Italianate-style columns, very little external detail, barely any landscaping and a colour scheme that would put anyone to sleep. The pre-reno value was $295,000.

AFTER

I had a tight budget of $30,000 to renovate the house internally and externally over nine days. Despite these limitations, I created a facade that now looks far less dated. While it's not going to win any design awards, it does look better than before. The ugly red bricks were rendered as part of the new colour scheme. Horizontal timber slats add detail, and basic landscaping including plants and paving paint completes the look. Post-reno value was $385,000.

Due to the tight budget, we couldn't afford roof spraying, so I organised a roof clean instead. This unfortunately really let the property down. Turn to the next page to see what the house could have looked like with roof spraying through a 3D digital render.

AFTER

To show you what a massive difference roof spraying makes, I've digitally altered the same house to show you what it could have looked like. The roof now complements and lifts the new external colour scheme, giving the property a finished look overall.

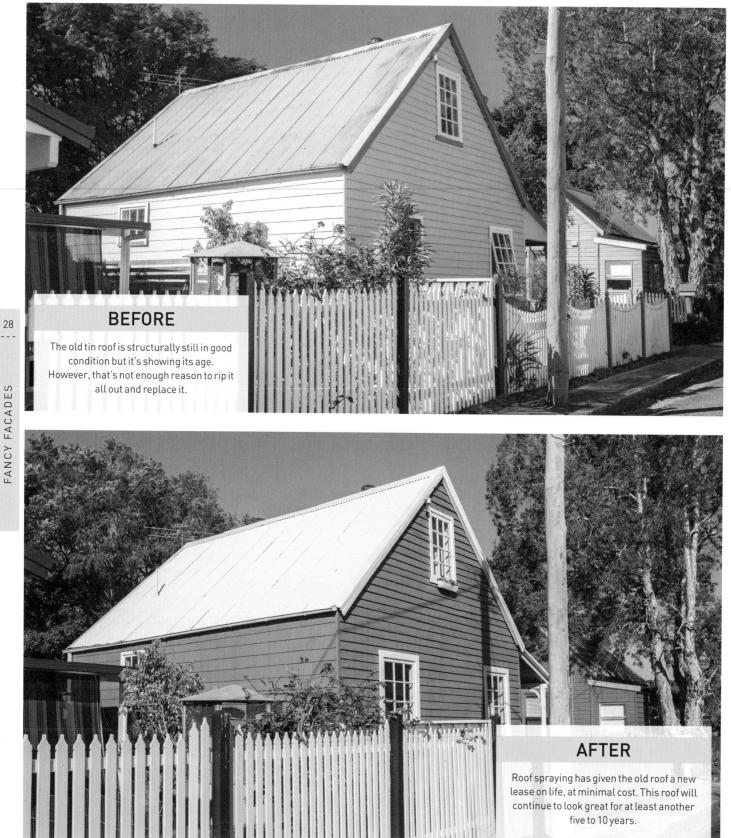

BEFORE

The old tin roof is structurally still in good condition but it's showing its age. However, that's not enough reason to rip it all out and replace it.

AFTER

Roof spraying has given the old roof a new lease on life, at minimal cost. This roof will continue to look great for at least another five to 10 years.

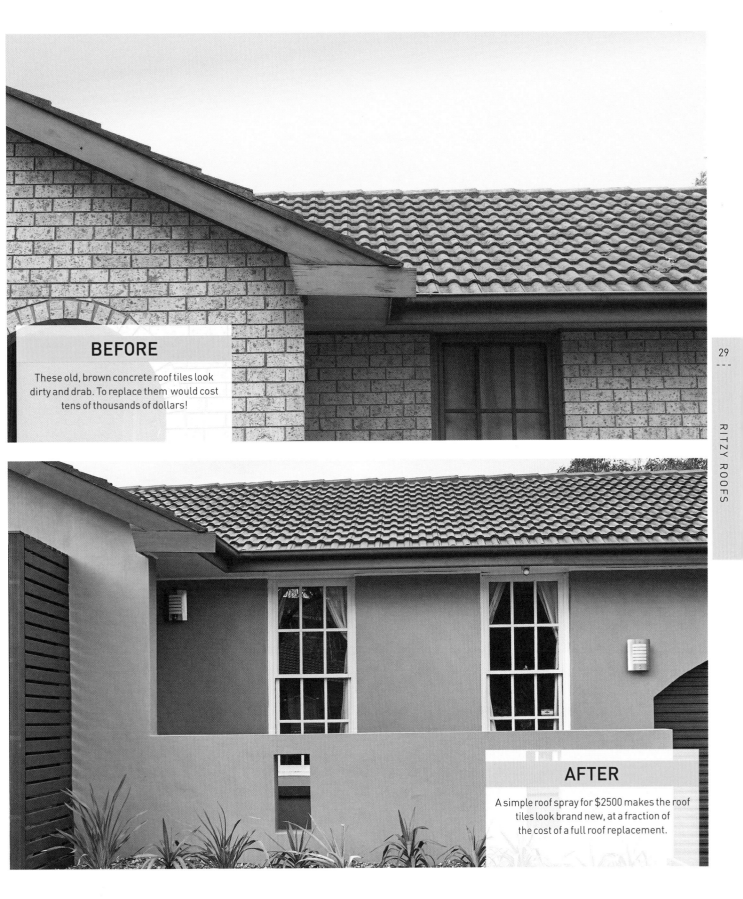

BEFORE

These old, brown concrete roof tiles look dirty and drab. To replace them would cost tens of thousands of dollars!

AFTER

A simple roof spray for $2500 makes the roof tiles look brand new, at a fraction of the cost of a full roof replacement.

RENDER SPLENDOUR

Rendering is a really clever way to instantly modernise a home when ugly or dated bricks are all that you see. A render, as the name suggests, is applied over your existing bricks or fibro exterior to transform the look of your house. Certain brands of acrylic renders can be coloured to match thousands of paint colours, eliminating the need to paint your external walls.

There are two types of renders: acrylic and cement. I recommend acrylic – it's flexible, which is better for expansion and contraction in walls, preventing cracks.

Rendering gives your facade a smooth, slick finish and works well on homes for which you want a modern, contemporary look. I know you probably know this, but I just need to say it ... you certainly would never render a beautiful heritage brick bungalow or other ornate brick home. Please keep that rule in your head about staying true to your home's architectural style.

A great budget trick is to do what I call a partial render – the facade only, and one or two metres wrapped around the sides of your house. You then paint the remainder of your bricks (to the rear section of your house) in the same colour as your front facade. This will save you a heap of money, yet gives your house instant street appeal. If you do have the budget, rendering your whole house is always the best way to go.

Asbestos buster

If your DIY project is a fibro-clad home, be aware that you're potentially dealing with asbestos. It's completely doable to render over the top of fibro asbestos with acrylic render. It encapsulates the asbestos rather than removing it (removal can be expensive). If you're not up to speed on where asbestos is lurking on your property, there are great websites on the topic.

AFTER

BEFORE

BEFORE

You gotta love ugly houses and this one is right up there. The batwing walls, hideous brown bricks and unruly garden make this house a renovator's dream. I snapped this one up for $550,000 before it officially hit the market. It pays to keep in contact with real estate agents!

AFTER

We concrete-cut the batwings off the house, rendered the facade only and added a simple new pergola at the front of the house to create a sense of entry. Colourful plants and lush new grass finished it off nicely. The whole house was renovated, inside and out, in 15 days for $67,500. My efforts were handsomely rewarded with a post-reno value of $690,000.

BEFORE

This home is a little ugly duckling that has never been shown any love. The yellow colour scheme is just as boring as the brown metal side fencing. Dirty roof tiles, plants in the wrong position, a relic of a letterbox and no front fence – this facade needed a lot of work.

AFTER

I had a budget of $10,000. The roof was high-pressure-water cleaned. What a difference! A bold new colour scheme on the walls and fencing instantly modernises the property. The biggest change was adding merbau timber to all trims, and building a pergola and front fence. To save money, I bought off-the-shelf fence panels. I added plants in the right spots so they don't visually block the entrance.

BEFORE

This coastal house wasn't looking very coastal! It was structurally sound, but cosmetically tired. The Italianate balustrade didn't match the setting, the driveway hadn't been cleaned in ages and the plants were a mess. It needed a classic Cherie reno!

AFTER

I only had $40,000 to renovate inside and out, including a new kitchen and bathroom. So I had to be economical on the facade. In went the render, followed by a lovely soft blue paint to give the house a coastal feel. I added a simple, decorative screen at the front to add interest, and I high-pressure washed the driveway. There wasn't any money left to buy plants, so I simply removed some of the existing ones and re-positioned others.

PERFECT PAINT

I love paint. It's every renovator's rabbit-out-of-a-hat move. It's liquid gold to any home. The reality is: paint can make or break your project.

Now, just so you understand me a little better, I need you to know that I am generally conservative with colour. When renovating a property, whether it's for selling, renting or investing, it's important to create the broadest appeal. And sometimes, crazy colour schemes can turn people away.

When it comes to your external paint, a good rule to stick by is to use **no more than three external colours**. But don't do just one, as you'll have no colour contrast. You can go for light or dark colours, depending on the style of your home – off whites, greys, browns and charcoals are good options, and you'll be inundated with choice.

Don't forget to make your colour scheme work harmoniously with your existing roof colour, unless you are roof spraying too. And for whatever colour you put on your walls, make sure you have a contrasting colour on your windows and all your trims. It's instantly appealing.

And here's where I contradict myself! But I'm allowed to, it's my book after all! I do believe in using a bold pop of colour on your front door. It's the place where you can inject some real personality. Go with whatever colour floats your boat – a joyful yellow, a fire-engine red, tangerine or teal – whatever makes you happy, but don't go fluoro!

BEFORE

BEFORE

I'm conservative with colour because I want my properties to stand the test of time. I don't follow fads or colour trends. This cute little inner-city home is looking a bit bland. Everything is in the right place, it's just that all the individual elements are showing their age.

AFTER

What a difference a lick of paint makes! By inverting the colour scheme, the home looks fresher and the windows now become a visual feature of the facade. Matching the paint colour of the front door to the pathways keeps everything looking cohesive. The front fence also looks much better now, all because of a new coat of paint.

BEFORE

Sometimes my budgets as a TV renovator are ridiculously small. But then again, a lot of home owners don't have a stack of cash in their bank accounts for renovations. I had $10,000 to transform this house, inside and out. That meant only cleaning up the facade, and not reinventing the wheel or performing major surgery in any way.

AFTER

I dragged out my spray gun and painted the whole facade and front fence in a soft light grey. I added timber architraves around the front windows and doorway to create bulk and scale, which I then painted in white so that they stood out against the grey.

The picket fence didn't match the theme of the house, so I got my carpenter to simply cut the tops off the pickets with his electric saw. That took about 10 minutes and cost me almost nothing in labour.

BEFORE

This house didn't look very appealing, and the front steps not being in line with the front door was a big no-no for me.

You want a home that feels welcoming, and that all starts with how people get to your front door. The balustrade enclosing the front porch makes it seem prison-like, and, like with a lot of unrenovated houses, the drab colours make the whole facade look dated.

AFTER

The roof was in great condition so I didn't need to make any changes there. I painted the whole facade and replaced the two Italianate porch posts with big chunky timber posts. My carpenter whipped up some matching merbau steps which we placed directly in line with the front door. This dramatically improved the friendliness factor and created much-needed symmetry. Adding basic plants softened the whole look.

BEFORE

This home's street front was letting it down in terms of kerbside appeal. The garden was threatening to take over the facade, blocking much-needed light from getting into the front of the house. And that green window awning is just ugly.

AFTER

A new coat of paint really brings out this home's weatherboard charms. Ditching the dirty old awning was one of the kindest things I could do. I replaced it with a simple timber decorative screen to help draw the eye away from the large first-floor window. The unruly growth in the front garden went to plant heaven, and low-lying plants took pride of place instead.

BEFORE

This house is an excellent example of the power of paint. The facade is tired and wouldn't make a positive impression at an open house. It all seems disjointed and neglected, which makes buyers feel like it needs too much hard work.

AFTER

A simple horizontal timber slat fence smartens up this home. I added a matching timber decorative screen to the front porch to maintain the sense of privacy while also creating an interesting feature. The driveway was in dire need of concreting so that was completed, and simple garden beds and plants now frame the house in the right places. The ugly terracotta roof was spray-painted in a complementary colour to the new external colour scheme.

BEFORE

This gorgeous Cape Cod–style cottage had great bones. The big let-down was the purple and lilac colour scheme. The previous owner loved it so much that she shared her paint with friends in the street – it was obvious where they lived! The landscaping was ramshackle and neglected, making the garden unuseable.

AFTER

I created a striking new look by using colour contrast to highlight the cottage's decorative elements. I added some simple timber fretwork under the balcony to re-introduce some of the original character which had been lost over time. I added planter boxes, with colourful plants, under the windows to make this home super cute.

GREEN THUMB THOUGHTS

Landscaping needs to be part of your plan from the get-go. The main reason to get started with the gardening is because it needs time to settle, which can happen while you get on with your interiors.

A luxurious lawn is the gold standard in real estate land and is a simple DIY job that most people can tackle. Do not, however, let all your hard-laid work get trampled over by big-booted tradespeople. Get some of that DO NOT CROSS tape and mark out the areas not to be walked on – you'll thank me later.

Your plant selection, once again, should all be tied to the style of your home. There are cottage plants and modern plants so don't plant the wrong type at your place. Cottages and weatherboard homes look a treat with softer heritage-style plants such as murrayas, lavenders, rosemary bushes and camellias. For modern places, think succulents, yakkas, sculptural cordylines and a whole lot more.

Timber sleepers are my number one landscaping go-to for cheap garden beds on a budget. Install them up on their edge (don't lay them flat) to add bulk and scale to your property. They come in treated pine, so you can spray-paint them the same colour as your house trims to make all external colours work together beautifully. If your budget allows, merbau garden sleepers look a treat, especially when you've used merbau timber elsewhere on your facade.

HOT TIP

Before your renovation starts, stockpile your newspapers. It's the poor man's (or, as I like to call it, the soon-to-be-rich renovator's) best gardening weapon for weed matting on a budget. Once you've popped your plants into your garden beds, completely cover your soil with newspaper. Then put your woodchips, mulch or pebbles on top of your newspaper. This stops weeds from growing in your garden bed. There, you just got your weekends back.

BEFORE

Never underestimate the power of good landscaping. This house shows exactly how an unkept garden becomes a waste of prime real estate.

The alfresco sitting area is a comedy show in itself, and the lacklustre shade sail looks like it could fall down at any moment.

AFTER

There was so much junk in this yard, it was incredible. It required a lot of hard work to clear this mess, but the result was well worth it. I removed one of the porch balustrades and got my carpenter to build some timber steps that now create an easy flow between the inside and the yard outside. Lush green grass and plants make this an inviting and usable space.

BEFORE

A mangled lawn, a path to nowhere and a creepy, old, rapidly dilapidating shed – who'd want to spend time in this backyard?

Everything looks neglected and in need of repair. It's certainly not somewhere I'd want to have a barbecue or let kids play.

AFTER

This was a low-budget reno, so I added a simple timber deck to help people transition from the inside to the outside. It also creates a nice neat area for entertaining and relaxing outdoors. We also demolished the shed out the back, which wasn't going to last too much longer anyway. The yard now looks so much bigger. New turf, of course, and the freshly spray-painted fences help to make this home's outdoor area great again.

BLING FLING

If you've got a balcony, always add a small table, a couple of chairs, cushions and a few decorative ornaments. It's such a beautiful way to set the scene, especially if you're planning to sell. It's a place people can see themselves in and it heightens the sanctuary element of your home, which helps people make that all-important emotional connection to your place. Even something like a gorgeous potted urn by your front door can make a world of difference.

Pathways and driveways need attention too. Don't go to the trouble of ripping up your old pavers: a simple blast with a high-pressure-water cleaner does it (a garden hose is just not going to cut it) and then a resurface with paving paint (see page 25). Once you've pressure cleaned everything, wait overnight for everything to completely dry, then apply two decent coats of paving paint in a heavy duty, non-slip formula.

Now here's a cautionary tale for you. I once paving-painted my own driveway. Unfortunately, the hardware store was out of matt paving paint, so I bought the gloss paving paint instead. One night, after a small dose of rain, I stepped out of my car and my leg slid forwards on the paving paint, right across the driveway. Instant splits, which I haven't done in 40 years. Youch! So, please always buy the non-slip, matt finish, just so you don't have to add physiotherapy bills to your overall reno budget.

Coming back to the topic of first impressions, did you know your mailbox and home numbers also count for a lot? Often, it is hard to find a decent letterbox. Sometimes you can find the right style but it's the wrong colour – in that case, just spray-paint it, to tie in with a colour on your facade. If you're handy with tools, you could even make your own, but we may be getting a bit too ambitious now.

For your house numerals, always go the stick-on option. That means no tradespeople required. Go smaller numerals, like a 50 mm size, for your letterbox and then something significantly larger on your house walls. Anything under 200 mm will be just too small to see from a distance. Do I need to say it again? I better just in case ... Make sure the shape and font of your house numbers suits the style and theme of your home!

And fences ... we dream about the white picket fence, but horizontal slat fences can look awesome too for houses that are chasing a highly modern look. Just never put a slat fence on a cute cottage house. And the good news is, buyers love fences. They provide privacy, security and they really frame a house. They really are the icing on the cake and don't need to cost the earth if you're smart!

BEFORE

This home was pretty cute already, but its awkward angles required some real strategic thought on my part. Best part of all, I had a big budget of $80,000 to play with. Jackpot! This meant I could move from budget to beautiful and take this facade to the next level.

AFTER

This reno took me a month to complete, but what a transformation! It looks like a completely different house. Raised, multi-tiered, brick rendered garden beds featuring exotic tropical plants and merbau decking edged with a merbau timber and wire balustrade makes the space inviting and visually appealing. I added a stone feature wall at the entry for a bit of wow factor, and a set of bi-fold doors encourages people to wander outside. This is one of my all-time favourites. Some days I amaze myself. Other days, not so much.

BEFORE

A double deck on this house ... what a bonus! While it's all structurally fine, everything screams dowdy and drab. There is almost no connection between the inside and the outside, and all that green shade cloth isn't making me green with envy.

AFTER

The biggest expense in this rear transformation was the addition of structural bi-fold doors. That zapped $15,000 out of my budget. But there was very little expense for everything else. I simply dragged out my trusty spray gun and painted the pergola roof, the balustrade and the house exterior, then I painted the old brown pavers with a paint roller. My carpenter added stairs to lead people down into the yard. My tenants now love this part of the house.

BEFORE

This was a tiny courtyard attached to a ground-floor studio apartment. It's not very functional or attractive, and it wasn't going to fit well with the internal renovation I was planning. I wasn't allowed to touch any common areas or walls due to strata regulations.

AFTER

Who doesn't love an in-built barbecue? The new bench seats provide a fun space for friends and family to sit, and the daybed is an ever-present temptation for relaxing the weekends away.

It's all low maintenance, with the exception that it needs a lick of timber oil once a year to keep the timber from drying out. The strong timber focus now ties in beautifully with the timber floors inside, achieving that seamless indoor–outdoor connection that adds real value.

BEFORE

Another classic example of a courtyard being used as nothing more than a dumping ground. This courtyard gives new meaning to ugly! These tiny spaces need big ideas to ensure you realise the maximum potential of the space.

AFTER

I removed everything, and I mean everything! I high-pressure-water cleaned the pavers and the back wall, then painted the wall in a strong colour. I added some cheap plastic screens to the back wall that I spray-painted in a copper colour for decorative effect.

My carpenters cloaked the old fences with merbau timber slats, and made matching bench seats too. The merbau timber definitely adds an element of luxury. I purchased some square pots, dwarf palm trees and off-the-shelf furniture, which took the space from drabulous to fabulous in just two days!

SEQUENCE OF CONSTRUCTION
Outdoor and Exterior Works

Start

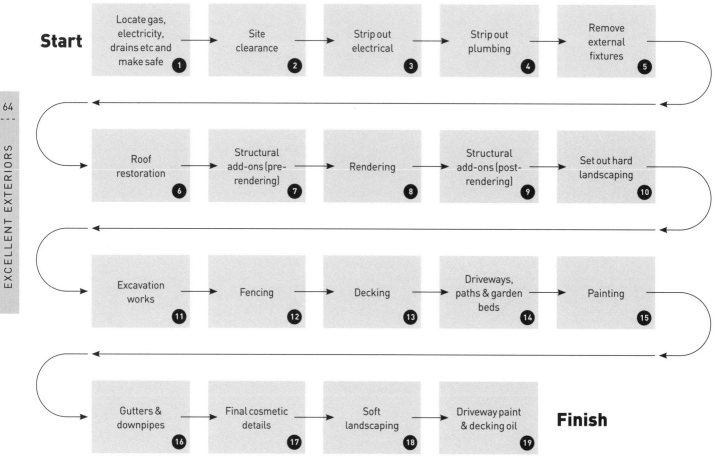

1. Locate gas, electricity, drains etc and make safe
2. Site clearance
3. Strip out electrical
4. Strip out plumbing
5. Remove external fixtures
6. Roof restoration
7. Structural add-ons (pre-rendering)
8. Rendering
9. Structural add-ons (post-rendering)
10. Set out hard landscaping
11. Excavation works
12. Fencing
13. Decking
14. Driveways, paths & garden beds
15. Painting
16. Gutters & downpipes
17. Final cosmetic details
18. Soft landscaping
19. Driveway paint & decking oil

Finish

AFTER

A simple cosmetic enhancement by one of my students, Trish Greening, shows that anyone can do this. Way to go, Trish!

BEFORE

CHAPTER TWO

LIVING LARGE

When I refer to the living zone I'm talking about the area that encompasses the lounge room and the dining and rumpus areas – but the lounge room is the jewel in the crown of this space.

For your lounge room to feel good it needs to have generous proportions, which is why buyers, renters and investors love the open-plan layout so much. It's just a more relaxed way of living. And families like connected spaces and enjoy room to move and the flexibility that it offers. Everything is less formal and much more casual.

A great lounge room is around 5 metres by 5 metres minimum, but the larger the better. The space needs to comfortably contain a lounge suite, coffee table, TV cabinet of some sort and, of course, a TV.

WONDER WALLS

If you're renovating an older house, you'll be well aware that homes were once made up of pokey spaces separated by lots of walls and doors. In years gone by, it was all about room segregation – a series of rooms in a home that didn't have any real connection to other rooms.

Mum used to be stuck in the kitchen all by herself preparing the meals, the kids would be either underfoot or separated off into their rooms, and the dad ... Probably reading the paper in the lounge room with his feet up, to continue on the stereotypes. Thank goodness times have changed, and so have the ways we use our home.

Due to work demands, families actually have less time together now that our lives are busier. Creating connection nowadays is super important and a good living zone should make this happen easily. Having a dining table that can double as a homework area or a kitchen bench for breakfasts allows families to interact more. Joining the dining area with the living space makes a lot more sense for how people really want to live their lives.

So if your living zone is stuck in the past, you're faced with knocking down a few walls internally to open up the space to create that open-plan living zone that we all know home owners, buyers and renters love.

With an internal change like removing walls, you may or may not need formal planning approval first. If the wall is **non-structural** (meaning it's not supporting your roof), there's a good chance you won't need to obtain formal planning approval from your local authorities. However, if the wall is a **structural** wall (it's supporting the roof), it's almost a given that you'll need to obtain planning approval before you demolish anything.

Unfortunately if you do need to get planning approval, it's likely to trigger a new set of costs like draughting of plans, a structural engineer and, of course, planning application lodgement fees. A few thousand dollars will fly out of your bank account in the blink of an eye, but it will still be worth it in the end.

If you're not sure if you need planning approval, simply call your local planning authority, ask to speak to a duty planner, and ask the question. They should be able to give you an answer over the phone.

DIY WALL REMOVAL

A lot of houses have tiny doorways leading from room to room. Quite simply, in the past, the different areas had no connection. Your home might have been nothing more than a series of rooms, clumped together under one roof. Nowadays the key is to widen those doorways or knock out whole walls to create a better flow internally. It may be an illusion of renovating but, when you knock out a wall or widen a tiny doorway, your internal space will instantly look bigger, even though the building footprint hasn't physically increased.

But that's not all. Nothing dates a home like arched doorways. And houses are full of them. Square those babies off, full stop. I call them the 'golden arches' and, trust me, they're not the good kind either. Get rid of them and widen doorways to make sure you can transition from room to room seamlessly. Repeat after me: NO MORE ARCHES.

LIVING LARGE

What you'll need

Reciprocating saw to cut plasterboard
Hammer
Crowbar
... and a lot of muscle effort

Before you start

Knock down the wrong wall and before you know it, you'll have the ceiling on the floor and your budget through the roof. First port of call before anything gets knocked down is a builder, carpenter or building engineer. They will help you determine if your wall is structural or not.

If it's a **structural wall**, you should <u>never</u> do this work yourself. Never! Call in a senior carpenter or a builder to handle the whole process for you. They'll need to install acrow props and a structural beam overhead, and then there is a heap of other carpentry tweaks to make sure that beam has been done to correct building code regulations. The average punter on the street wouldn't know where to start so this is definitely one of those tasks that you should <u>never</u> do yourself.

If, on the other hand, the wall you want to tear down is a **non-structural wall**, it's party time. As the wall is not supporting anything, it should be fairly easy to do this job yourself. But, before you get started: see my hot tip opposite!

How long will it take?

A couple of hours. Demolition is hard work!

Cost

If you're removing a non-structural wall, the good news is that the cost is minimal. Most of it will be demolition, which only requires the effort of your muscles, not necessarily your money.

HOT TIP

Before you demolish anything or cut into your walls with a reciprocating saw, make sure you isolate all the electricity to **OFF** at your mains electrical switchboard. I've seen tradespeople saw through electrical wires behind walls – it's not a pretty sight.

BEFORE

AFTER

FABULOUS FEATURE WALLS

After you've widened your space and improved the flow between rooms in your living zone, it's time to add a bit of character to this area. Enter stage left: the statement wall. I like a strategic focal wall as a feature wall. It lifts the space with a bit of character and defines it. The best homes add a feature wall that's interesting without being overbearing.

There's a lot of stuff going on in your lounge room, so your feature wall should be relatively low key. Paint is a renovator's best friend and the cheapest way to create a feature wall on a budget. The big question is – what colour should you choose?

There are thousands of paint colours. In an ideal world, your home will have one consistent wall colour through all your rooms, and no more than three feature walls located in your whole property.

Your feature wall colour needs to be a complementary colour to your main wall colour. That means no wacky or way-out shades. Resist the urge to think you're on a renovation TV show. Wild colours look great on camera, but not in your home.

In an ideal world, you should try and link your feature wall colour to your lounge room furnishings. For example, the images opposite are the lounge room in one of my properties. The living zone has stone-coloured walls with a retro-inspired brown-and-white wallpaper. It's a beautiful wallpaper that adds visual interest and something extra to the room, however, you'll notice it's not a crazy print.

You can see from the photos that I have a brown lounge and walnut furniture, which ties in with the wallpaper. I've then used some pops of colour containing yellow that tie the room together. This is the principle you need to follow when choosing your feature wall paint or wallpaper.

BEFORE

Oyster light, tick! Old ratty carpet, tick! Off-white walls, tick! This room has all the elements that I often see in my pre-reno spaces, and the result is pretty uninspiring. But I've got a few clever tricks in my bag that will transform this dated, two-bedroom apartment into a chic and inviting space.

AFTER

The trick here is the flooring – I used DIY laminate floorboards that are easy to install. This added instant appeal to the space. Then there's my feature wall in dark blue that picks up the tones in the flooring. So the room is interesting but also still in harmony. And check out the lighting: a nice new pendant light and some seriously sexy standing lamps next to the couch. And just like that, the room looks a million times better, without spending a million dollars!

BEFORE

There's no doubt, this room has been lovingly looked after. It just needed some easy cosmetic lifts and new furniture to make the space look contemporary and cool. The biggest challenge was the awkward proportions, but with a little bit of wow-factor wallpaper, I knew I could make this room sing.

AFTER

I didn't want to lose the retro feel of this apartment, so I opted for classic furniture that still ties in to the mid-century mood. Flipping the living and dining sections has made the awkward proportions of the room work so much better. But the shining star is that wonder wall. The wallpaper is a subtle pattern with a chocolate-and-white fleck that is unlikely to date, and that fabulous starburst mirror just brings the styling to life. And it was all achieved on a tight budget too!

BEFORE

I've said before that I'm not into wild colours, but there is a time and a place for a wash of cool tones in a room. Before I got my hands on this home, it was a 'plain Jane' property that lacked life or soul. I needed to give it some personality.

AFTER

Two shades of blue give this home a heartwarming feel. This property was pitched to a younger buyer, so it needed to attract that market segment. Well, great news – it sold immediately with two buyers battling it out, and the purchase price set a new suburb record for a renovated house. Happy days!

BEFORE

Mottled carpet, big heavy curtains, dated pendant lights. Sometimes it's hard to know where to start. But I knew that something pretty wonderful was possible – I just had to get more light and air into the space.

AFTER

The look-at-me wallpaper is the absolute hero in the room. The pendant light in the corner picks up on the pattern in the wallpaper design and lights up a pokey space – double win! Add new flooring and furniture that 'floats' off the ground and the space suddenly looks very modern and luxe after only a few days of hard work.

WHAT LIES BENEATH

So your walls are now looking good, but what about the floors? Don't underestimate the impact flooring has on your property's overall look and feel. My rule of thumb is to be consistent with flooring throughout your home. And ideally that means one flooring type throughout, with the exception of your bathroom and laundry, which should always be tiles.

So which flooring is best? Tiles, floorboards, floating floors, vinyl? None is really better than the other statistically, but what I do know is that floorboards are the preferred flooring type for most buyers and renters alike – everyone loves them. They're a timeless look, can take a bit of a beating, the upkeep is super easy and they add real warmth and softness to a room. There is a trend for wider boards but normal-size boards around 90–120 mm in width are perfectly fine and more affordable.

Be aware that thousands of floorboards exist. Walk into any flooring store and you won't know where to start looking, let alone how to narrow it down to one. It's important you know there are three different floorboard types:

1. **Laminate**
2. **Engineered**
3. **Hardwood**

Each of the above types of floorboards comes with its own pros and cons.

Laminate floorboards are the cheapest flooring option. You can get these types of boards supplied and installed by most flooring supply stores for around $50 per square metre.

For any property over $750,000, engineered or real hardwood floorboards are the way to go.

For **engineered floorboards**, supplied and installed, you'll be looking at around $100–$130 per square metre, depending on which flooring store you go with.

For **real hardwood floorboards**, you're roughly looking at $150–$200 per square metre.

HOT TIP

Laminate floorboards hate water. Never install these types of boards in bathrooms or laundries. If you do, they'll buckle up and you'll need to rip them up and replace them. Laminate floorboards are used commonly in properties with lower property values under $750,000.

TILES

Of course, tiles are also an option for flooring, but they can get incredibly cold. So be aware of where your house is located. Tiles really work in warmer climates, or for homes near the beach or regional properties where dust is more common.

FLOORBOARDS: WHAT TO CONSIDER

Type of floorboard	Pros	Cons
Laminate	Man-made floorboards with various layers. Cost effective, durable, easy to clean. Can be installed over existing flooring. Can be laid by you or by a flooring installer.	Badly made versions contain formaldehyde. Not water resistant, which can cause floorboards to rapidly expand and buckle (requiring replacement). Cannot be sanded if scratched or worn.
Engineered	Man-made floorboards with various layers. Easy to maintain, can be sanded back, but only marginally. Can be stained and painted. Easy to clean. Long lasting and great for family homes. Can be installed over existing flooring. Good middle-of-the-road option.	Almost double the cost of laminate flooring. DIY installation is possible, but only if you are reasonably handy.
Hardwood	Real timber floorboards. The king of all floorboards. Can last a lifetime if you look after your boards. Can be sanded and polished numerous times. Aesthetically pleasing and the preferred flooring option for most people.	Expensive to buy and install ($75–$120 per square metre, plus carpentry cost for installation and sanding. The installation is time consuming). Susceptible to termite damage if there is no adequate protection in place.

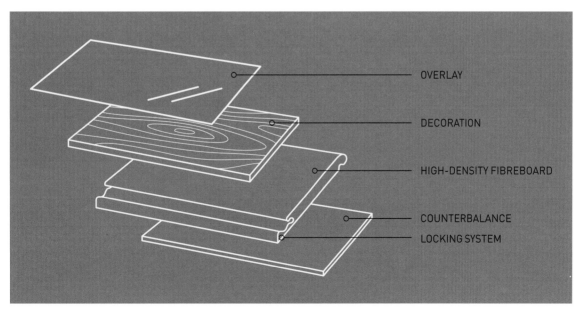

OVERLAY

DECORATION

HIGH-DENSITY FIBREBOARD

COUNTERBALANCE

LOCKING SYSTEM

A typical example of how laminate floorboards are constructed.

BEFORE

Where to start with this pattern-frenzied room? Brown bricks and tiles NEVER mix. This room is an eyesore, but it's oozing with potential. The dark and heavy decor needs some lightness to lift this room and make it a space where you can relax.

AFTER

Look, there's nothing wrong with using patterns, you just don't want it to dominate a space. So I used a graphic rug to pull the room together and toned back the walls and floors with a soft grey palette. It didn't cost the earth, and it's now a lovely soothing space. New curtains add to the subtler and more gentle style that makes everyone feel calm.

HOT TIP

If you've decided to tile your floors throughout your home, always go for larger, not small tiles. 300 x 600 mm tiles are my preferred floor tile size. They make your property appear larger than it really is. Small tiles on your floor will make your space seem smaller. Also, never highlight your grout as a feature on your floors. Always colour-match your floor tile grout to a colour as close as possible to your floor tile so the grout lines disappear on your floor!

DIY PAINTED FLOORS

The good news is, you may have existing hardwood floors already in your home but they're looking a little drab. There's no need to rip them out – just stain or paint your floors instead. This can look really great in cottages or homes with dated pine flooring.

What you'll need

150-grit sandpaper
Vacuum cleaner
Detergent
Mop
Masking tape
Primer
Paint roller
Paintbrushes
Mineral spirits
Lots of polishing rags
Polyurethane-based porch and floor enamel

Get started

1. Scratch up the surface with 150-grit sandpaper, by hand or using a sander. This will help the paint adhere to the floor. Then vacuum and mop the floor with a detergent cleaner and get rid of any little specks that could get trapped under the paint. Let it dry out completely.

2. Use painter's masking tape to seal off skirting boards, doors and door frames so that paint from the roller or brush does not flick onto them.

3. Apply a primer suitable for your paint type using a roller and paintbrush for the corners of your room, then let it dry overnight. For a professional finish, wipe the floor over again with mineral spirits, using tack cloth or a rag.

Paint perfection

4. The floor is now ready for the first, thin coat of paint with a roller. For corners, it's a good idea to cut-in a short distance (about 3–5 cm) from the skirting board or wall with a brush as the roller won't get into the space. Roller at least two more thin layers and allow at least 24 hours between coats. You'll work faster if you have heat on to dry as you go, but please wear a mask and keep those windows open because of the paint fumes.

How long will it take?

About three days.

Cost

Under $500 in materials. Most of this is DIY effort, labour-wise, which costs you nothing but your time.

HOT TIP

Don't plan to stay in the house
while the paint is drying and
keep the windows open for
ventilation.

PRIVACY ISSUES

There's a little trick I like to add to properties that have privacy issues at their front door. You know those homes where you step from the front door straight into your lounge room? A lot of basic homes have this exact layout and it all feels a bit too soon, don't you think? There's a quick and easy solution – add in a timber privacy screen.

The set-up

It's best to get a carpenter to do this, and it should only take three hours or less to complete. With most carpenters at under $70 an hour, you will only rack up a couple of hundred in carpentry costs.

What you need

Your carpenter will measure your space and install the screen. 90 mm by 45 mm slats of pre-primed pine, often called designer pine, is the best material to use. The slats can be painted to any colour you like. You can typically buy them for under $10 per lineal metre.

The great thing about this screen is that it provides a visual break between your front door and the main room, so the lack of privacy is less of an issue. The vertical slat–style allows light to pass through and therefore doesn't darken your room. And best of all, it looks a little bit flash for not much cash!

BEFORE

AFTER

There was nothing structurally wrong with this room – it had great bones. The new screen beside the front door makes all the difference to this space. It creates a sense of privacy, and effectively separates the entryway from the living area. A beautiful soft colour scheme makes it look so much better!

BEFORE

BEFORE

There's a pretty amazing window in this room, but you wouldn't know it thanks to the heavy furniture and old curtains and blinds. The front door opens directly into the lounge room, which buyers and renters hate, so I need to strategically knock that objection out of the water.

AFTER

This is a property for which I've done a 3D virtual renovation. I would get my carpenter to erect a simple timber slat screen that lets light in but provides much-needed privacy between the front door and the lounge area. I'd drop a feature light in front of that screen to add a bit of wow-factor and mood lighting. I'd ditch the carpet and install floorboards instead. A flash new colour scheme will have this lounge room looking super-duper, in next to no time.

LIGHT HEARTED

If you're faced with an older-style home then you'll be well accustomed to the fact that flat, lifeless 'oyster' lights used to be the number one choice for ceilings back in the day. My advice? Get your electrician to rip 'em out.

Recessed downlights are definitely the way to go. They sit flush with your ceiling, are unobtrusive and look great in any style of home. Ideally, always opt for LED, not halogen, because they're longer lasting, cast better light, are cheaper to run and don't emit as much heat. They're also environmentally friendly and that's what we should always aim for in everything we do.

There's also room for a little bit of feature lighting in your lounge room. I love a beautiful pendant light, but I don't recommend you stick one in the middle of your living space. It can be distracting and will take up visual space towards your TV. My top tip is to stick a feature light to the right or left side of your feature wall. It adds something extra to your room for a small cost and it can double as mood lighting!

Always install circular downlights, not square ones. It's impossible to keep the square downlights in a perfect grid-like pattern. Over time, they'll look messy.

HOT TIP

Always opt for satin chrome downlights, not polished chrome. Fingerprint marks on your polished chrome downlights are never attractive. And never use white-framed downlights. They look significantly cheaper than the satin chrome ones, yet cost the same.

AFTER

One of my favourite tricks is to place a pendant light in a dark corner of the room. I never really like them dangling in the middle of a space, but off to one side is visually beautiful and adds a rockstar element to your statement wall. Soft, natural, earthy colours soften the room, making it warm and modern.

BEFORE

Pokey kitchens have just got to go. We don't live like that anymore, and it's seriously one of the biggest turn-offs for buyers and renters. The trick, however, is in making a living space and a kitchen work together from a visual point of view.

AFTER

A lighter colour scheme, without harsh bold colours, always works well in living and kitchen zones. The new custom kitchen cabinetry, in a high-gloss polyurethane finish, was tinted the same colour as the walls, and contrasted with a white stone benchtop. Everything looks like it belongs together. The big win here was removing the high breakfast bar, which cut the space in two. In doing this, I freed up space for a little dining area. It all looks so much bigger now, even though the dimensions of the room didn't change. The new chrome downlights illuminate the space beautifully without being obtrusive.

COLOUR ME HAPPY

Because the living area is a room where lots of people with different tastes will spend time together, you need to stick to a safe colour scheme. My absolute favourites are neutrals like stone shades, greys, whites and tans. I really hold back on the colours for all my rooms and then add in texture and pattern through the smaller, decorative pieces such as ornaments and soft furnishings, like lounge cushions. To dress up your lounge room, you can use colourful blanket throws on your sofa, a gorgeous printed rug on your floor and great artwork on your wall that has complementary colours to all your furnishings.

I know it's a trend at the moment, but I usually would not do dark walls in a living space, unless it was very large. Generally, it messes with the light in the room, for one, and secondly, it makes it feel less spacious. Always remember that your objective when renovating internally is to lighten and brighten your rooms, not make them darker!

You could use a darker tone as a feature wall, though. For this to work, you want your colours to subtly work together. So your darker wall should be a similar tone to your main wall colour, but stronger – double, triple or quadruple the tint for the best results. Promise me – no purple walls if you want to sell your place!

You also need to keep in mind that the room will have to accommodate a lot of hard-working furniture. Sofas, armchairs, coffee tables, TVs, storage units – it's all got to fit somewhere! Make sure your pieces are scaled to fit perfectly with the size of your room. If you have a large space, a three-seater sofa will look great, as opposed to a two seater that might seem too insignificant for the space and vice versa.

FURNITURE TIPS

For a room to really work, you need clever pieces that don't absorb light and space. The key is to not clutter your space.

Your first decision is where to put the TV. The rest of your pieces will fall in line from there. Ideally, you'll have a windowless internal wall to set it on, then the couch can sit opposite it.

I also like a lower-backed sofa, which increases the sense of space. Grandma and grandpa's big fat plush sofas are not the way to go (though they are super comfy to sit on).

Another great idea is to have a sofa that sits off the ground on legs, rather than a hard solid lounge that goes all the way to the floor. Again, it adds a feeling of airiness to your room .

Opt for open furniture. Enclosed coffee tables are far too heavy, so go for one that has thin open legs. Glass coffee tables look great too, and are perfect for increasing the sense of space in a small living room.

You can ditch the armchair if you don't have space, or go for something very minimal.

BEFORE

This room really doesn't require a lot of money to be spent to make a big difference. The problem here is the colour scheme. It was straight from the 1990s, complete with blue picture rails cutting the walls in half. Oh, and the very dated cornice wallpaper frieze brings back memories of my own mum doing this to every room in our family home. But that was very much then, and this is now.

AFTER

This contemporary reno was incredibly budget-friendly. I used my usual trick of painting the walls, removing the picture rails and replacing the carpet with inexpensive Calcutta marble–look tiles. Stylish and slimline furniture further enhances the room's light and airy look and feel.

BEFORE

There are just so many don'ts in this room. So it obviously needed a complete cosmetic overhaul. But you know me, I was going to do it all on a shoestring budget.

AFTER

I'm so proud of how beautifully this room shines now, thanks to some fabulous furniture and a super-sleek colour scheme. Those pillars and the fussiness were all removed, and the ceiling and surrounding walls were painted white, while my feature wall has a luxe-looking wallpaper treatment. A net curtain lets light filter into the space, and feature lights over the dining table add a little pizazz.

BEFORE

It helps to know the elements that have the most impact in your home – and in this case it's the arched wall leading into the dining room, the patchy orange-and-brown carpet and the stained walls. To the untrained eye, this home isn't worth much at all. But when you're in the know, a transformation can add enormous value.

AFTER

Square off the arches, rip out the carpet and paint those walls, and guess what happens? A completely new room! This is one of my favourite examples of the power of a cosmetic renovation. Note the darker feature wall in the dining area that elongates the whole space.

FINE DINING

When linked to your lounge, your dining area needs a bit of attention. The defining piece is, of course, the dining table. Ovals work well because they add some nice curves into the space, without the harsh corner edges. I also like a beautiful big rug under a dining table to define the space. And please, when you're measuring it out, leave enough room so that when you pull chairs out, they still sit on your rug. There's nothing worse than a rocking chair that sits half on and half off a rug. Measure that out!

The dining space is a great spot for a fabulous pendant light that hangs right over the centre of your dining table. And sometimes, the space looks really great if you extend the pendant lower than you normally would. Open spaces can make a dining area feel a little lost, so using a rug and a light to define the space brings back a little intimacy.

BEFORE

AFTER

Now this is a dining room of which you can be proud. Please note how the rug easily and completely accommodates the table and chairs, even when they are pulled out. The pendant lights above the table add a sense of place to the room, and the dramatic black highlights are minimal so they don't dominate the space.

BEFORE

Who doesn't love an open-plan space? The only problem can be bringing all the elements together – the living room, dining room and entry area. It can be a busy space, and sometimes it's hard to envisage the end goal, but that's the beauty of thinking about everything you do before you actually start.

AFTER

With the kitchen and staircase being so dominant, I broke the space up into zones, which are defined by large rugs. I haven't cluttered the space with too much furniture, and all the items I chose are floating, so it doesn't create heavy blocks anywhere.

Off-the-shelf green curtains bring the outside inside, and decorative wallpaper and feature lights turn the ordinary into the extraordinary. I now rent this house out on Airbnb, and everyone who rents it never wants to leave!

BEFORE

This dark, dank and unappealing dining room isn't really going to get anyone's appetite going. The linoleum flooring is the first offender, but the dark wood-panelled walls are pretty awful too.

AFTER

You light up my life! This room now sings, and it was just a simple matter of removing the flooring and polishing those floorboards. I also painted over the wood-panelled walls and the ceiling to lighten the room. Suddenly, you have the kind of space where you'd want to host Sunday lunch!

TIME TO PLAY

Sunrooms

You gotta love a sunroom. It's the multi-functional room in your home that not all of us have. A reading room, sitting area, kids' playroom or hardcore gym even, this room can be whatever you want it to be. Often located at the rear of your house, most sunrooms get a decent amount of sunlight (that's why they're called sunrooms …) that allows you to feel the warmth of the outdoors, with the comfort of being indoors. Sunrooms have a tendency to be more lightweight in construction and will be really easy or difficult to renovate, depending on how flimsy or solid your room actually is.

Do they add value? My oath. Trick them up the best way you can, but don't spend a fortune. And before you spend any money, make sure the room complies with minimum head height requirements so they are formally classified as a 'habitable room'. You don't want to be dropping money into something that's a dead duck, so check with your local planning authority first.

In all my years of renovating experience, it's the floor in your sunroom that's likely to cause you the most angst. As many sunrooms were once an outdoor area, there's a moderate chance there will be water leak issues somewhere. Seek the help of a local builder to have a look and sort this out for you. If you don't, it could play havoc with whatever flooring you choose to install.

Rumpus rooms

It's official: if you have a rumpus room, you're not living in a small inner-city terrace where you can't swing a cat. Chances are you're out in the suburbs with a larger, newer house. Rumpus rooms didn't exist back in the good old days. They became popular in the 1970s and have stuck around ever since.

But what is a rumpus room? It's not your lounge room or sunroom, although its uses can be very similar. It's your recreation room, the noisy part of your house where you play games, watch TV, have parties or let the kids play. A true activity zone! This room tends to be larger sized – it's not uncommon for it to be at least 5 metres across each side to cope with all the activities that take place here. And, surprisingly enough, it's a room that tends to have windows in plentiful supply, maybe because this room is almost always orientated to the back of your house. In some countries, rumpus rooms tend to be in your basement.

As renovators, these rooms don't need a lot of strategic thought and tend to be on the more neutral side, simply because you're likely to have so much colourful stuff in them anyway (think games, crayons, artwork). Your flooring material should be your biggest concern. Get one that is easy to clean (think spills), so floorboards or tiles are the best way to go. You'll need good light, like any other room, so simple recessed downlights are the way to go. A lick of paint and you'll be done!

BEFORE

What an ugly sunroom! It looks as though you'd catch a disease if you walked on that carpet, and the pink vertical blinds are criminal!

AFTER

What a turnaround. You'll be surprised to know that this room required minimal effort, yet it looks so different. I simply removed the drapes to let in the light, I painted the walls and I installed a new ceiling fan and some recessed downlights – which means you can now use this room day or night. Walnut floating floorboards top it off.

BEFORE

Rumpus rooms in basements often don't have ideal layouts. And what I knew for sure is that this room would never win any design awards. Never. Ever. This was a low-budget property and I had almost no money to renovate it ... but I do enjoy a challenge.

AFTER

I dragged my best friend out of hiding – that's my spray gun – and together we tangoed around the room in a mist of paint, all the same colour, except for the floors, which I painted in a dark concrete shade. It's still not going to win me any design awards, but you've got to admit, it does look better than before. Best of all, it only cost me $200!

BEFORE

There are a few other areas of your house that you should not neglect during a renovation – staircases and hallways! This reno brings back memories of a home owner I worked with on one of my early TV renovations. She had installed this carpet 12 months before the reno and didn't want to rip it out. I told her it was all wrong and it had to make a trip to carpet heaven. And so we disagreed. Back and forth we went …

AFTER

I stood firm on this one, and rightly so. Her brown open-pile carpet was darkening the tiny staircase and made the steps harder to see. I installed a closed-loop carpet with a textured pile that actually cost less than her original carpet. It's a great example of the power of your finishes when buying your renovation fixtures. When the new carpet was installed, she could see I'd made the right decision. Sometimes people need a little convincing.

BEFORE

This is Nanny's house. She lovingly kept it in tip-top condition, but never had a need to modernise it. These sorts of houses are a renovator's dream come true because structurally, they are spot-on. The bones of the entry here are especially good. It's just cosmetically tired.

AFTER

A soft baby blue welcomes you as you step in the front door. The questionable carpet was removed to expose gorgeous floorboards underneath, which my floor sander simply polished. The brown bottled-glass doors were introduced to my bin, and a beach-style ceiling pendant light now connects this home to its coastal location.

BEFORE

Really, do I need to say anything about this entryway? It would send any cub scout running for the hills if they knocked on this door. I look at it and feel like I'm in a trance (not that I have ever experienced that ...)

AFTER

Hello beautiful! All I did was paint the walls black and wallpaper one wall with a striking but cost-effective wallpaper (just $60 a roll, and I only needed one roll). You don't need to go to university to do this. And this is why I love renovating: sometimes the smallest things make the most impact.

CHAPTER THREE

KILLER KITCHENS

So, we've come to the kitchen, which just happens to be the most important room in your home for adding value ... No pressure!

The heat is on because this room has so many elements and is heavily used every day. Given how hard this room has to work, it shouldn't be a surprise that a well planned and executed kitchen will add enormous value to a home.

Basically, this room is your money maker, according to bank valuers – it's the one room they pay particular attention to (along with your bathroom). These two rooms also happen to be the most expensive to renovate, and rightly so. They have a lot of stuff in them!

BUDGET BRAINS

For your kitchen, **allocate a budget of no more than 2 per cent of your home's current property value**. Not what you bought the property for, but what it's worth today. If you don't have any idea what your property is worth, simply look at real estate websites for local comparable sales.

For example: if your home is currently worth $600,000, your kitchen renovation budget should be no more than $12,000, fully finished, inclusive of all materials, fixtures and fittings and trade labour. Everything, basically! If you're disciplined enough to stick to this formula, you'll greatly minimise your chances of overcapitalising.

Once you've set your budget, breathe easy ... I've got some great money-saving ways to make your kitchen look great, without costing the earth. I'm all about maximum impact with minimum spend. And that doesn't mean bad quality either. You should take immense pride in the quality aspect of any place you're renovating. It is, after all, someone's home.

Believe it or not, you can transform an entire kitchen for less than $2000. I've even done a fully finished kitchen makeover for just $991! See my kitchen reno on pages 124 and 125 for a kitchen that was transformed for just $2021. So I don't want to hear any excuses, OK?

AFTER

This kitchen was renovated on a minuscule budget of less than $1500. I simply swapped the laminate benchtops over to timber. I laminate-painted the base cabinets a funky new colour, added some low-cost Ikea accessories, a simple venetian and a chunky light. It's the little things that count.

BEFORE

AFTER

BEFORE

Brown timber everywhere. The owner of this home couldn't bear to throw this kitchen out. You see, it was her wedding gift, from her late husband, who built it for her with his bare hands. Aww ... where can I find a man like that? While it would have looked great in its day, it's now looking more like a sauna! Somebody get me a towel.

AFTER

The power of paint is beautifully demonstrated here in this refreshed and renewed beauty. I laminate-painted the cupboards, resurfaced the benchtops and stainless steel–painted the rangehood. Vinyl floor planks completed the look, all done for just $993. This kitchen is now suitable for steaming veggies, not yourself. And we still keep hubby's memory alive.

WORK WITH WHAT YOU HAVE

First things first. If your kitchen layout is good but your kitchen looks drab, a simple cosmetic update might be all you need to bring your kitchen back to life.

Start with the cupboards. How are they looking? If the cabinetry is a terrible colour, you can easily paint those babies back to beautiful again. Laminate paint will be your new best friend.

BEFORE

So much yellow. While this might have been the height of fashion at some point, the colour of this kitchen was really showing its age. I knew I had to drag my bag of cosmetic tricks out. Work it, honey ...

AFTER

This spring chicken now sparkles from top to bottom, after a budget-busting makeover. I did this one with my younger sister, Jeneane, in just two days for $2021, inclusive of brand spanking new appliances.

DIY CUPBOARD PAINTING

What you'll need

Electric drill or screwdriver
Tile and laminate cleaner or a mild detergent
Cleaning cloths
Scourer (scratch resistant; only if required)
Epoxy putty (only if you have holes to be filled)
Adhesive (only if required)
Dust respirator
240-grit sandpaper (or electric hand sander)
Masking tape
Plastic drop sheet
Disposable gloves
Tile & laminate primer
Paint stirring sticks

2 paint trays
Foam mini roller & frame
38 mm paintbrush
Laminate paint (which you can tint to any paint colour)
600-grit sandpaper

PAINT CALCULATION

To calculate how much paint you'll need, multiply the length of your cabinets by their height to give you your square metreage. Then divide that amount by 12 to give you your required amount of paint in litres. If you're painting the inside of your cabinets too, don't forget to add that amount to your calculations. Most kitchens only consume 1 or 2 cans of primer and the same amount of laminate paint.

Formula: (Length × height of cabinets) ÷ 12 = Total litres required.

BEFORE

HOT TIP

Laminate paint is in a satin finish. If you want high-gloss doors, you simply substitute laminate paint with tile paint, which has a high-gloss finish.

AFTER

BEFORE

AFTER

Get ready

Step 1: Clear everything out

Move items such as your fridge and anything on your kitchen benchtops out of the way.

Open a window or two for ventilation.

Step 2: Remove handles

Remove all your kitchen cupboard handles. The fastest way to do this is with an electric drill. Alternatively, use a manual screwdriver. It is often recommended that it's best to take all your cupboard doors off your internal kitchen carcasses before painting them. It's not required. If you do this, you'll probably need to bring a handyman or carpenter in at the end to put all your cabinet doors back on and align them correctly. This will just add to your cost. You can successfully laminate-paint your cupboard doors without ever having to remove them.

Step 3: Clean like crazy

Thoroughly clean and wipe dry all of your kitchen cupboards with tile and laminate cleaner. Alternatively, a mild detergent can be used. Avoid any other heavy chemical cleaning products as they could react negatively with your laminate paint. Your cabinet doors need to be squeaky clean – scrub them with a cloth or, if necessary, a scratch-resistant scourer. No dirt, dust, kitchen grease, soap scum, mildew or anything else is to be left on your cupboards (otherwise it will show up under your laminate paint).

Step 4: Fill dents

If there are any chips or dents in any of your doors, use epoxy putty to fill these imperfections. It is a fast-drying product that you can sand shortly after application. If any of your laminate is coming off your old cabinet doors, simply anchor these parts down by using a strong adhesive, like spray adhesive. If you have any badly damaged doors, look to get those replaced by a cabinet maker. Once fitted, you can then laminate-paint over to match all your other painted doors.

Get set

Step 5: Sanding

Once your kitchen cupboards are free of all debris, it's time to start sanding. It's best to wear a dust respirator to avoid inhaling any fine particles. The fastest way to sand all your kitchen cupboard doors is with an electric hand sander. To sand an average kitchen by electric sander, it will take about one hour and they're less than $50 to buy at major hardware stores. Alternatively, you can do it the harder way, by hand, with 240-grit sandpaper (likely three to four hours' sanding time).

Start sanding all your cabinet doors, inside and out, in a circular motion. Don't forget to sand the left, right, top and bottom sides of your cabinet doors too. If your old kitchen doors have a gloss finish, this needs to be completely removed by sanding it off thoroughly.

Please note: You only need to lightly sand/etch your doors (except where you have a heavy gloss surface) to enable the laminate paint to bond firmly to your cupboard doors. It is not a heavy sanding process.

Once you've finished sanding all your cupboards, wipe them with a slightly damp cloth. Your cupboard doors must be squeaky clean and thoroughly dry before you can start the next step.

Step 6: Masking

Mask off any surfaces that you don't want to get laminate paint on. For example, your oven edges and any wall surfaces that your cupboards back onto. If you're not painting the insides of your cabinet doors, mask around the edges on the back of your doors so any paint applied to the front of the cupboards doesn't leach over onto the back of your doors.

Use a good-quality masking tape because cheaper masking tapes (tan coloured) must be removed within 24 hours, otherwise adhesive residue starts bonding to your surfaces and is difficult to get off. Put your plastic drop sheet (or newspaper) on your floors or any surfaces that you don't want to get paint on.

And go

Step 7: Undercoating/priming

Put on your disposable gloves and open your can of tile and laminate primer. This is your primer/undercoat, which helps your laminate paint bond properly to your cabinet doors. Stir thoroughly with a paint stirring stick, mixing in a circular fashion from the bottom of the can upwards, to ensure the primer is mixed properly. Pour the primer into your paint tray. Do not pour too much into your tray, otherwise it will make it more difficult to roll excess paint off your roller.

To apply the undercoat, do one cabinet door at a time. Use a mini foam roller but also have a paintbrush at hand to cut in any edges or get into any tight spots that your roller can't reach. It's best to roller all the edges of your doors first (top, bottom, left, right), then roller the front and back of your cupboard doors.

Apply the primer in a zigzag pattern for good adhesion. Once you have your door completely covered in paint, do not load your roller up with primer again. Just roll back over your door, in one direction, from top to bottom, for the best finish. Never press down too hard on your roller.

Undercoat all your cabinets, front and back, applying a thin (but not too thin) amount of primer. Do not put too much primer on your cabinet doors as this will cause the paint to appear slightly thickish and will result in a substandard finish. Wait four hours for the primer to completely dry. In the meantime, wash your roller in water and dry it with an old towel or cloth.

Please note: You need to work quickly when working with tile and laminate primer as it tends to dry quite quickly (in about 30 to 60 minutes, especially on a hot, humid day). Try to minimise your paintbrush use wherever possible. The more you can use your roller, the better your finished result will be as you don't see paintbrush strokes with rollers.

Step 8: Sanding

Once dry, lightly sand all your cabinets again with 240-grit sandpaper. Do not sand too much as you don't want to take any of the primer off. This is a very quick process – it should take no more than five to ten minutes to do your whole kitchen. Wipe over/dust off your cabinets again with a dry cloth to remove any loose particles.

Step 9: Laminate paint

Open up your can of laminate paint. Remember, you can tint laminate paint to any colour you like. Your local hardware store can do this for you. Mix your paint in the same fashion as your primer. Stir thoroughly with a stirring stick, mixing in a circular fashion from the bottom of the can upwards, to ensure the paint is mixed properly. Pour your laminate paint into your paint tray, but not too much!

To apply the laminate paint, simply repeat the same process as applying your laminate primer, doing one cabinet door at a time. Paint all the edges of your doors first then roller the front and back of your doors. Apply the laminate paint in a zigzag pattern again. Once you have coated your door in paint, do not load your roller up with paint again. Just roll back over your door, in one direction, from top to bottom, for the best finish. Never press down too hard on your roller.

Again, use your roller as much as possible, not your paintbrush. Paint all your cabinets, front and back, applying a thin amount of paint (but not too thin). Wash your roller in water and dry with an old towel or cloth.

Your cabinets will be touch dry in two hours but you shouldn't apply your second coat of laminate paint until six hours later. Most people wait overnight to apply their second coat of laminate paint, and I would recommend doing this.

Step 10: Sanding and second coat

The next day, once again, lightly sand all your cabinets, but use 600-grit (not 240-grit) sandpaper. Do not sand too much as you don't want to take any of the paint off. Wipe over/dust off your cabinets again with a dry cloth to remove any loose particles. Apply the second coat of laminate paint as you've done previously.

Allow your cabinets to dry for at least eight hours but be aware that laminate paint takes at least one week to achieve its maximum hardness. You need to treat your cabinets very delicately and not vigorously clean any of your surfaces during this curing time.

Step 11: Clean Up

Remove all masking tape off all surfaces. Put your cupboard handles back on.

BEFORE

HOT TIP

Keep your doors and drawers slightly ajar so the paint doesn't dry them shut.

AFTER

BEVEL BE GONE

Back in the 1970s, we were in love with the bevel. It was all the rage, the cool thing to have. But now, it's as dated as they come. What were we all thinking? It gives great meaning to not following the fads!

A lot of old kitchens around the country have beveled doors. But it's not a good reason to rip your old kitchen out. You're going to love this little trick of the trade. If your old kitchen doors are still in great condition, simply cover up the bevel instead. Hire a good carpenter for a day to nail a medium density fibreboard (MDF) or pine timber moulding straight over the top of the bevel. This will give you a shaker-style door with no bevel to be seen anywhere. You then laminate-paint all your doors.

EMBARRASSING MOMENT

Talk about embarrassing. I was filming my USA TV show, *5 Day Flip*, when the producer asked me to nail in a timber moulding to all the old doors in an otherwise plain kitchen.

You see, I'm not a carpenter but in this instance, they wanted me to look like one. 'Do you think you can nail in those trims, Cherie?' the producers asked ... 'Sure!' I chanted.

The cameras were rolling, I looked like the Lara Croft version of renovators; life was good. All done and I'm feeling pretty proud of myself, thinking carpentry ain't that hard after all.

About an hour later, when we moved on to another task in the kitchen, the head carpenter went to open one of the doors. It wouldn't open. Then he tried the next one. Shock, horror, it wouldn't open. I had nailed every door shut. Embarrassing!

Moral of this story, don't pretend to be good at something when you're not! Know when to DIY and when not to DIY!

On the flipside, the doors looked fabulous!

BEFORE

This room would be right at home in a timber cabin, off somewhere in the woods. Unfortunately, it's way off course and found its way into a suburban family home.

AFTER

I installed a new kitchen but everything here is budget: flat-pack kitchen cabinets that we assembled ourselves to save money. Off-the-shelf benchtops and stick-on marble floor tiles kept the budget down.

The transformation of this kitchen proves that even the worst sideshow can make it to the main stage, after a complete renovation, inside and out.

BEFORE

This kitchen was obviously a loved and well planned out member of this family home. Everything in this kitchen is right, layout wise. It's got a decent amount of cabinets, benchtop space is in plentiful supply and the window lets in lots of natural light. It just works on so many levels. The only issue was its slightly dated appearance.

The reality is, this kitchen is borderline. You could take it or leave it. You could keep it as is, for another five years, and it would still be OK. However, my plan was to renovate the rest of the house so I knew if I didn't update the kitchen, I'd probably regret it later, for not maximising my property value.

AFTER

All of the kitchen cabinets were in great condition so there was no need to dump those into landfill. I simply called on my trusty cabinetmaker to make me new doors, drawers and end panels only. They cost me $1,540 for supply only and my carpenter installed them in one day. I bought all my laminate benchtops from a benchtop factory, which my carpenter also installed. Brand spanking new appliances topped it all off. It now looks like a new kitchen but it's not. Best of all, it was done at a fraction of the cost of replacing a whole kitchen from scratch.

HEAVENLY HANDLES

Do you know what else can make an enormous difference? Cupboard handles. Hardware stores have an entire aisle dedicated to them, and you can pick up some easy-to-install ones that will instantly modernise your kitchen.

But don't go too crazy on the style – no fancy curved or bow handles, OK? Your kitchen cupboard handles should stand the test of time. I'm a huge fan of satin chrome or brushed nickel T-handles, which you can get from any hardware store. They don't leave fingerprint marks behind and they'll still look modern in 20 years' time.

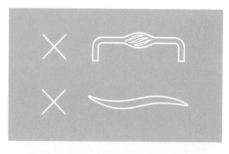

STEER CLEAR OF OVERLY DECORATIVE
OR CURVED HANDLES

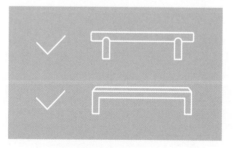

FOR A MODERN LOOK OPT FOR SLEEK
SATIN CHROME OR NICKEL HANDLES

CHERIE'S SAVING TIPS

Be aware that the way you buy stuff will dictate what price you pay for your materials. When renovating for profit, bulk formats are the way to go. Smaller or individual sizes cost more.

Let's take a simple example – your cupboard handles. The average kitchen typically contains 30 to 40 handles. If I buy an individual simple chrome T-handle, it'll cost me $7.20. If I buy the bulk project pack of 10 handles (exactly the same handle), it'll cost me $23.00. That means I pay $2.30 per handle instead of $7.20. If I buy individually, it costs me more than double the price!

Individual Handle: $7.20 each	Project Pack of 10: $23
Handles Per Kitchen: 30	Handles Per Kitchen: 30 (3 Packs Required)
TOTAL COST TO BUY: $216	**TOTAL COST TO BUY: $69**

Saving: $147

Copper-coloured T-handles give your kitchen cabinetry a luxe feel.

BENCHTOP BRILLIANCE

It's highly likely that your benchtop is in need of a bit of love too. Don't lament over an old laminate or timber benchtop. They can be costly to replace. If you make the decision to rip 'em out, you'll need to call in an electrician to disconnect your cooktop. You'll need to call in a plumber to disconnect your sink. And in comes a carpenter, too, to pull out your ugly old benchtop and install a new one, then the electrician and plumber come back again to reconnect everything. You've just cost yourself a stack in labour costs.

My best tip here is to keep your old benchtops and just resurface them instead. I'm in love with benchtop transformation kits for a resurfacing finish you never thought was possible.

It's surprisingly easy to apply and it is a very similar process to laminate paint. Check out my step-by-step video on how to benchtop resurface by jumping on **www.renovatingforprofit.com.au**. You'll find a five minute instructional video there that will have you benchtop resurfacing like a pro, in next to no time. You'll spend a weekend doing it, but boy will it be worth it! Check out my before and after pics!

BEFORE

Look at this gorgeous kitchen. There's absolutely nothing wrong with it (structurally, that is). The colour scheme? Well, that's another story.

AFTER

A lick of laminate paint has totally transformed this room. You'd never know the peach-and-yellow horrors that lie beneath. I simply added feature tiles on one side to give it some life. And the benchtop looks great, all thanks to paint!

DIY COUNTERTOP RENOVATION

What you'll need

Rust-Oleum countertop transformation kit

Kit includes: base coat, 2-part protective top coat (parts A & B), diamond-embedded sanding pads, 6 inch by 0.4 inch (150 mm by 10 mm) nap roller, 6 inch (150 mm) high-density foam roller, paint stirring sticks.

You will also need:

**Epoxy putty (only if you have
 holes to be filled)
Dust respirator
Cleaning cloths
Detergent
Masking tape
Plastic drop cloth
2 mini paint trays
1 inch (38 mm) paintbrushes
6 inch (150 mm) roller paint frame
600-grit sandpaper
Lint-free cleaning cloth
Disposable gloves
Mixing container
Mineral turpentine**

Get ready

Step 1: Clear everything out

Move anything on your kitchen countertops out of the way. Open a window or two for ventilation.

Get set

Step 2: Sanding

If applicable, fill any holes in your countertop surface with epoxy putty and let it harden.

Proper sanding of your countertops is extremely critical with this product. A diamond-embedded sanding pad is contained within your Rust-Oleum kit. It's best to wear a dust respirator when sanding to avoid inhaling small particles. Sand your countertop (including the sides) by hand, in a circular motion. It takes an hour or two to sand an average-sized kitchen. If your old countertops have a gloss finish, ensure you completely de-gloss them by sanding extensively. If you do not sand your countertops sufficiently, the paint may not adhere properly and therefore affect the product's performance. Once you are done sanding, thoroughly wipe down and clean your countertops and remove any loose surface particles. Your countertops must be squeaky clean and completely dry before you proceed to step 3.

Step 3: Masking

Mask off any surfaces that you don't want to get countertop paint on, for example around your kitchen sink and on your backsplash tiles, and lay down your plastic drop cloth.

And go

Step 4: First coat – base coat paint

Open your can of base coat paint. This is your countertop color. You cannot tint this product to a different color. Stir the base coat thoroughly with the paint stirring stick. Always stir from the bottom of your can upwards. Ensure you only use the base coat paint when the air (ambient) and surface temperature is 61–85°F (16–29°C) and the relative humidity is below 85 per cent.

Pour a portion of the base coat paint into a clean paint tray.

With a paintbrush, cut in/paint around your benchtop edges and especially tight places around your cooktop and sinks first. But, try to quickly roll over your paintbrush strokes using the nap roller that comes in the kit. Doing this removes any visible signs of brushstrokes.

Once you've cut in all your benchtop edges, roll an even level of the base coat paint over all your benchtop surfaces, always working in small sections at a time. Once you've coated a small section of your benchtop in base coat paint, do not load up your roller with paint again. For the best finish, just roll back over your benchtop, in one direction, from top to bottom. Never press down too hard on your roller.

Continue painting the remainder of your benchtops, in small sections, applying a thin to medium amount of paint (not too thin but not too thick either). When you are done applying the base coat, check that you haven't missed any sections.

Wash your nap roller in water and dry it with an old towel or cloth.

Wait for two hours, until your benchtop is touch dry.

Please note: Try to use your nap roller as much as possible, not your paintbrush.

Step 5: Sanding

Lightly sand your benchtop in between paint coats, using 600-grit sandpaper. Do not sand too much as you don't want to take off any of the paint. This is a light and quick sand, purely to remove any surface impurities. Wipe your benchtops thoroughly with a clean, dry cloth to remove any particles.

Step 6: Second coat – base coat paint

Wipe over/dust off your cabinets again with a dry cloth, then apply your second coat of base paint, in exactly the same fashion as your first coat.

Allow your benchtop to dry overnight before you apply your protective top coat.

Step 7: First coat – protective top coat

Your protective top coat is a gloss surface that helps protect the base coat paint on your benchtop. This comes in two cans, Part A and Part B, which will need to be mixed together. One is the gloss coating and the other is the hardener, which starts activating the moment the parts are mixed together.

Don't forget to wipe down all your benchtops with a lint-free cleaning cloth to remove any dust that may have settled on your benchtop overnight.

Wearing gloves, precisely measure out half the contents of Part A and Part B, respectively. If you put too much or too little of one part, the gloss coating may fail. Pour these two liquids

together in a mixing container, thoroughly stirring for at least two minutes with a paint stirring stick. It's important to stir this product really well to ensure proper activation and adhesion.

Once mixed, pour the blended protective top coat mixture into a clean paint tray. You'll need the remainder of parts A and B later, for the second coat of your protective top coating, so ensure you close the cans well. If you don't do this, you'll need to buy a whole new kit to get more of the protective coating, as this part of the product is not sold separately.

IMPORTANT

Once Part A and Part B are mixed together, the working time is only four hours. Do not use any leftover protective top coat after four hours as the performance of the product will have greatly diminished.

With a paintbrush, cut in/paint around your benchtop edges and especially tight places around your cooktop and sinks first. But, try to quickly roll over your paintbrush strokes using the foam roller that comes in the kit. Doing this removes any visible signs of brushstrokes.

Once you've cut in all your benchtop edges, roll an even level of the protective top coat over all your benchtops, remembering to always work in small sections at a time. Once you've coated the surface in the protective topcoat, do not load up your roller with paint again. For the best finish, just roll back over your benchtop, in one direction, from top to bottom. Never press down too hard on your roller.

Wash your foam roller in mineral turpentine and dry it with an old towel or cloth.

Your protective top coat will be tack-free in four to six hours. However, I highly recommend you let your benchtop completely dry overnight before you apply your final coat of protective top coating.

Step 8: Second coat – protective top coat

For your second and final coat, simply repeat the steps from step 7.

Step 9: Clean-up and curing

Carefully remove all masking tape. Allow your protective top coat to dry for 48 hours for light use. Wait seven days for full cure and maximum stain resistance.

SPLASHBACK SPLENDOUR

Your kitchen splashback is the area around your walls near your sink, cooktop or other benchtop space that protects your walls from greases, water splashes and all other general food preparation mess.

People use all sorts of building materials in this space – think coloured glass, faux brick, stone, mirrors, but the most popular splashback material is, without question, tiles. And yep, you've probably got wild and wacky tiles from the 1970s too. Hopefully they're structurally in great condition, just the wrong colour. Good news – there's no need to rip them out. Just tile-paint instead.

Now, tile paint ain't no ordinary paint. It's specialty paint with magical ingredients that are formulated and designed for the paint to stay on your tiles, for years to come. The key with this sort of product is good surface preparation and following instructions. See page 163 for more information on tile paint. It took me a year or so to work out the best technique. I learned the hard way, you don't have to!

Your splashback doesn't need to be boring. It's definitely a little place where you can inject some colour, pattern or creativity, without it costing you a tonne of cash.

Tiles are a fail-safe option and, with thousands of tiles around, your mind will boggle with too much choice. For more expensive properties, you can extend your engineered stone or natural stone benchtops up into your splashback area too. Mirrors and toughened glass (remember: it needs to be tempered, heat-resistant glass) are a super inexpensive way to add a luxe look into this space and one of my little magic tricks is to use wallpaper behind tempered clear glass for true splashback splendor! See page 147 for an example of this. The splashback looks like tiles but it's simply wallpaper with heat-resistant glass over the top!

AFTER

I think tile paint is a miracle product, but only if you know how to apply it right. I can't stress enough the importance of good surface preparation. If you do it right, it will last for years and years.

DIY WALLPAPER SPLASHBACK

What you'll need

Wallpaper
Measuring tape
Pencil
Level
Wallpaper paste
Bucket
Paint stirring stick
Paint roller tray
38 mm paintbrush
Wallpaper smoother or squeegee
Utility knife
Clear heat-resistant tempered glass
    (available from any glazier, made to your
    required custom size)
Glass cleaning spray and newspaper
1 tube of clear silicone
Masking tape

Get ready

Step 1: Calculate your wallpaper

Measure the length of your splashback wall to be wallpapered. Divide the length of your wall into your wallpaper roll width.

For example: If your splashback wall was 3600 mm wide and your wallpaper roll width was 580 mm, your splashback wall would require 6.20 strips (3600 ÷ 580 = 6.20), which would round up to 7 strips of wallpaper at whatever height your splashback is.

Step 2: Smooth surface

Make sure your wall is clean and smooth. That means no lumps or bumps in old plaster or previous paintwork. If required, sand your wall, then remove any dust and particles.

Step 3: Get a straight line

To start your first wallpaper strip, you need to draw a straight vertical pencil line using a level. This will ensure your wallpaper goes on straight and does not end up sitting on an angle. I suggest you draw your starting line at least half a wallpaper strip in from the edge of one wall. Alternatively, you can draw your starting line in the centre of your wall and work your way outwards.

Get set

Step 4: Wallpaper paste

Your wallpaper paste packet will have instructions on how to get the best consistency. In a bucket, add the paste to the required amount of water. Then mix this with a paint stirring stick until the paste has a nice thick consistency. Pour a small quantity of paste into your paint roller tray.

Use your paintbrush to apply your wallpaper paste to the corners and outer edges of your splashback, then coat the rest of your wall, ensuring a nice consistent film over the entire area.

And go

Step 5: Get the hang of It

Line up the edge of your first wallpaper strip with the pencil line you've drawn on your wall. Push your wallpaper into position with your hands. Grab your wallpaper smoother/squeegee and smooth out any creases or bubbles by pushing those out from the inside to the outer edges of your wallpaper. Do this gently so you don't tear or damage your wallpaper. This process also helps your paper stick to the wall.

Repeat this process for all your other strips of wallpaper, overlapping the edges if needed. Once all the wallpaper is applied, trim the wallpaper edges off with a utility knife, using the straight edge of your wallpaper smoother or your spirit level to get a straight line.

Step 6: Cover it up

Give your wallpaper a day to dry, then grab your tempered heat-resistant glass. Clean the side that will sit against the wallpaper thoroughly before you place the glass against the wall. It's best to clean glass with a good glass cleaner and newspaper, not a cloth. Cloths tend to leave lint behind. If your glass is not cleaned properly, it will show.

Move your sheet of glass into position, being extremely careful not to chip any of the corners. You may need a second person to help you lift the glass into position. Run a bead of clear silicone around the edges of your glass to hold it in position. You may need to apply a few strips of masking tape over the glass and onto another surface to hold the glass in position until your silicone dries overnight. Once dry, remove all masking tape. Clean the front of your glass, then stand back and be amazed!

RAVISHING RANGEHOODS

Now that your cabinetry and benchtops are looking all fresh and fancy, you might find your old rangehood is really letting the team down. Yes, you can scrub those things and de-grease them like crazy, but another little trick I like to add into the mix is resurfacing your old white or brown rangehoods with stainless-steel paint.

This is a specialty paint that creates a rich, metallic finish. It provides an easy and affordable way to modernise your rangehood, rather than ripping it out and replacing it. When you rip out your old rangehood, your new one often won't be exactly the same size. Today's appliances are much smaller than they were a decade or two ago – you'll be left with weird gaps, which won't look great. So, to avoid all those troubles, keep your existing rangehood and just refresh it instead. It'll look a million times better and the paint is quick and easy to apply.

HOT TIP

The more coats you apply of stainless-steel paint, the more stainless steel looking it becomes!

BEFORE

Don't get me wrong, I love copper items like feature lights or even cupboard handles. But not so much in my rangehoods. It's dated, it's dirty, and it needs to go.

AFTER

Replacing this rangehood would've been costly and, due to its vintage dimensions, it would have been nearly impossible to find a new model that fitted exactly in its place. Thanks to some nifty stainless-steel paint though, it now sits perfectly in sync with the rest of this revamped kitchen.

BEFORE

AFTER

DITCH THE OLD

The reality is that your old kitchen may be too far gone to fix: rotten doors, warped shelves, everything falling apart. If you're thinking about starting from scratch with new cabinetry and benchtops, you're going to have to pull out the old.

Now the penny-pinching begins. If you're pulling out a dated (rather than worn) kitchen, you can easily sell it online – there are heaps of websites and online portals. Yes, one man's trash is another man's treasure! You may get $500, $1000 or more (depending on how big or good your old kitchen actually is), so don't instantly reach for the sledgehammer and smash it to pieces.

You can even advertise your old kitchen to include DIY removal too – which is an ideal way to save you some grunt work and put a little bit back in your kitty. The trick here is not to be too greedy. You really want to sell your old kitchen, so price it reasonably and add strict terms for pick-up and payment.

BEFORE

IN WITH THE NEW

The cost of a new kitchen can spiral out of control pretty quickly. It can balloon past $10,000 to $30,000, without you even blinking an eyelid. So, it pays to be a good researcher, or at least buy a book by a good researcher: me!

3 WAYS TO GET A KITCHEN INSTALLED

1. DIY, and bring in specialist trades as needed.

2. Get a cabinetmaker to do most of the installation.

3. Hire a kitchen showroom company to handle the whole process for you.

Option 1 is the cheapest option, option 2 is middle of the road and option 3 will be the most expensive (at least double or triple the cost of option 1; but it may be the safe path to go if you're completely clueless about construction).

I'm a big fan of a flat-pack kitchen. And there are plenty of good ones around in your major hardware stores or at some big furniture shops. There are now online companies that have whole businesses dedicated to flat-pack cabinetry alone!

You can save money by assembling the cabinetry yourself (if you can assemble Ikea, you can assemble any other flat pack) and then paying a carpenter to professionally install all your cabinets and benchtops. An experienced senior carpenter should be able to do the work in two days. Most carpenters are on $40 to $65 per hour inclusive of GST. Eight hours a day multiplied by two days = 16 hours × $65 per hour, so budget around $1000 for your carpentry bill.

And be aware that there are **two kinds of flat-pack kitchens** to choose from:

1. Standard sizes, which generally come from large hardware stores or large retailers.

2. Made-to-measure flat packs, for more precision. Have a look online for options.

KILLER KITCHENS

AFTER

The kitchen is a flat-pack kitchen. Do you think anyone would notice? Nope.

CHERIE'S TIPS FOR
FLAT-PACK FABULOUSNESS

1. Measure, measure, measure. The whole project depends on your digits, so get it right. Get it as precise as you possibly can and always get a second person to check your measurements before you order.

2. You'll still need professionals. Have a good carpenter, plumber, electrician and tiler (for your splashback) ready to go. These tradespeople are worth their weight in gold. Plus, they'll get it done faster than you possibly can.

3. Buy yourself an electric drill. You will be able to assemble your cabinets in a fraction of the time spent doing it manually with a screwdriver or Phillips head.

4. Flat-pack kitchens are well suited to any home under $750,000 in value. Any property over this amount warrants custom-made cabinetry with snazzier surfaces on your cabinetry doors.

5. Finally, if everything starts to go wrong, call in the professionals before you go any further.

BEFORE

Step right up! See the world's smallest kitchen, before it's too late! You'll be amazed at the lack of bench space, horrified by the disjointed flooring and you'll be truly appalled by the bright-green cabinetry!

AFTER

I installed a new kitchen but everything here is budget: flat-pack kitchen cabinets that we assembled ourselves to save money. Off-the-shelf benchtops and stick-on marble floor tiles kept the budget down. The owner even made his own feature light!

The transformation of this kitchen proves that even the worst sideshow can make it to the main stage, after a complete renovation, inside and out.

ALLURING APPLIANCES

Appliances are the icing on the cake for any kitchen renovation, particularly to incoming owners if you're selling – they don't want to see crusty old ovens and dishwashers. But, as with most things in the kitchen, your appliances can make or break your budget. Big tip – focus on the finish. For me, it's stainless-steel appliances all the way.

They look great with any colour scheme, they're timeless and they look significantly more luxurious and expensive than standard white appliances, even though they cost the same. White appliances just look cheap and nasty and fewer people buy them nowadays.

BEFORE

Is this a kitchen or a thoroughfare? No one seems to want to stop and pause too long in this space and I can't say that's a surprise. Dark and uninviting, this room needs a total overhaul starting from the ground up.

AFTER

A whole new world! With more storage than before and some shiny new appliances, this kitchen makes you stop and pay attention for all the right reasons. Cocktails anyone?

BEFORE

AFTER

CHAPTER FOUR

BATHING BEAUTY

Yes, it's the smallest room in the house, but it's also one of the most important.

A shabby, pokey, mildewy bathroom is one of the biggest turn-offs for any prospective buyer. But it honestly doesn't take all that much to turn your bathroom into a shiny space that makes you feel clean just by looking at it – and that is going to add value to your home.

SMALL SPACE, BIG IMPACT

Although small in area, your bathroom is a room that adds big value according to property valuers. So this room is all about strategy. Most typical bathrooms are around 2 metres in width by about 3 to 4 metres in length, which is around 6 to 8 square metres at best.

And yes, you have a lot of stuff to fit in there. Of course, the essentials are a bath, shower, toilet, vanity and accessories – fitting them in while making this room functional and practical will take the best planning skills you have.

For the tiny space that it is, the bathroom is one of those rooms where costs can easily blow out. A full bathroom renovation will call for a lot of specialty trades to be coming and going and plenty of fixtures to be installed along the way. Roughly speaking, the average bathroom renovation cost is $10,000 to $15,000, all said and done.

It's a common renovator mistake to rip out a perfectly good bathroom that could have been left as it was, with just a few cosmetic lifts and tucks required instead. Yes, there are lots of hideous bathrooms out there with wild and wacky tiles but, once you take a closer look, you'll see that structurally, you might have one in great condition.

CHERIE'S BATHROOM RENOVATING TIPS

Before you get started, think about:

– whether your reno is going to be warts and all, ripping out what you have and starting again

– or if your reno could be less invasive and consist of a budget-friendly revamp instead.

BATHING BEAUTY

AFTER

TERRIBLE TILES

Not many people know that you can do a really good bathroom refresh for around $1000. Yes, you read right! And best of all, if you're organised, you'll be able to cosmetically refresh your crappy old bathroom in just one weekend. **The key is to know when to leave good enough alone**.

If you've decided not to go crazy with the sledgehammer and are going to leave everything in your bathroom as is, you'll be pleased to know there are a few great tricks you can use to make your bathroom appear newer.

The botox of the bathroom revamp world is **tile paint**. You buy this in small cans from any major hardware store. Make sure to use tile paint in conjunction with primer, an undercoat that helps your tile paint bind to your tiles. Specialty paints like this can save you a stack of cash because it means you don't have to rip out and replace your old wall tiles. When you remove tiling, you often end up damaging the waterproofing membrane on your floors and walls, which means more cost because you'll have to re-waterproof the space. By keeping all your old wall tiles and painting them instead, you can save $1000, straight off the bat – just paint over those ugly old wall tiles and you can almost pretend those pink patterns never happened! Tile paint is perfect for wall tiles only.

So, I hear you scream: 'But I have hideous floor tiles too!' Never fear, there are specialised floor tile transformation kits available, too. Check at your local hardware store. These products are similar to the tile paint you use on your walls, but have a slightly different application process and components. **Remember**: you cannot use normal tile paint on your floor tiles!

Also remember, tile paint will give a glossy, shiny finish to your tiles. If you want your tiles to be a matt finish, you can substitute tile paint for laminate paint instead. What most people don't know is that both products are the same; the only difference is the finish.

HOT TIP

You can tint tile paint to any paint colour. Simply pick up your tin of white tile paint from the shelf in any major hardware store, go to the paint mixing station and the staff there will tint your tile paint to whatever colour you want.

BEFORE

You've got to love it when people combine brown and salmon as their colours of choice. While the colours in this bathroom were from a time gone by, luckily there was nothing wrong with the layout, except the lack of storage (often an issue in bathrooms).

AFTER

I had the choice in this project to go bold or go home. Obviously, I chose the former and went all out with colour (the owner's favourite) through tile painting. By placing a feature colour on the rear tiled wall and adding mirrored storage, the space felt so much larger and more uplifting. It's now the perfect place to unwind at the end of a long day.

BEFORE

Oh look ... someone went on a tropical holiday and was inspired to create this cream-and-green dream on their return. Oversized bathtubs like this are never a good idea and take up way too much floor space, not to mention the giant feature plant (TREE!). It's leaving very little room for the owners to move around. But with no budget to rip everything out, cosmetic Cherie came to the rescue.

AFTER

The bathtub would have been a HUGE expense to rip out and move, so I simply updated the fixtures and fittings and tile-painted for a fresh, new look. The tree went into the backyard where it belonged, along with the resort-style towels.

BEFORE

There was just so much wrong with this little project. No wonder there's no mirror to reflect all that ugliness. Floral wallpaper (kill me now), curtains, a plastic vanity, the list goes on. Thankfully, the layout was spot-on and no plumbing changes were required.

AFTER

You'd be forgiven for thinking this was a completely different bathroom. The wall colour alone makes a whopping big difference, as does the tile paint. This photo was taken before the mirror was put on, but it now reflects a sleek and modern space that won't date for another ten years.

BORING BATHS

Know a good thing when you see it? For me, that is the granddaddy of all bathroom fixtures, the big old porcelain baths that many older homes have in place. I'm not talking about those fancy claw-footed porcelain baths (though they're fantastic and super cute too). I'm talking about those big, solid, recessed square porcelain bathtubs that take a team of strong men to carry them out. Never rip one of those out; it's criminal if you do. If you're completely changing your layout, can I convince you to keep and re-install it in your new scheme?

In days gone by, they built stuff to last – and porcelain baths retain heat in a way that newer, less expensive acrylic baths can only dream about. The only problem is that, after a few decades of wear and tear, porcelain baths can look discoloured and worn. But nine out of ten chances, they are now just the wrong colour.

Say hello to another great product: tub and basin paint. You'll find it hiding in your local hardware store.

Be aware that it's pretty stinky stuff due to the hardening activator that you mix with the paint, and it requires specific conditions in terms of the room temperature you need to apply it at. Think of this paint as the difficult diva of all cosmetic refresh products. However, put up with the attitude and you'll have a great, new-looking bath – see the images opposite. It'll cost you under $300 (you'll have to buy two or three packs). Simply apply a few layers to your tub over the course of two to three days (follow the packet instructions). Lighter baths may need two to three coats, while darker-coloured bathtubs may need three or four coats. Remember, only one coat per day.

If the thought of getting down and dirty with this product doesn't float your boat, you'll be happy to know that you can call in the resurfacing professionals to do it for you. It will be a few thousand dollars and it's definitely better quality than the DIY version. You have options!

HOT TIP

Buy yourself a good respirator with this product or you'll have one cracker of a migraine each night! A flimsy dust respirator is not going to cut it.

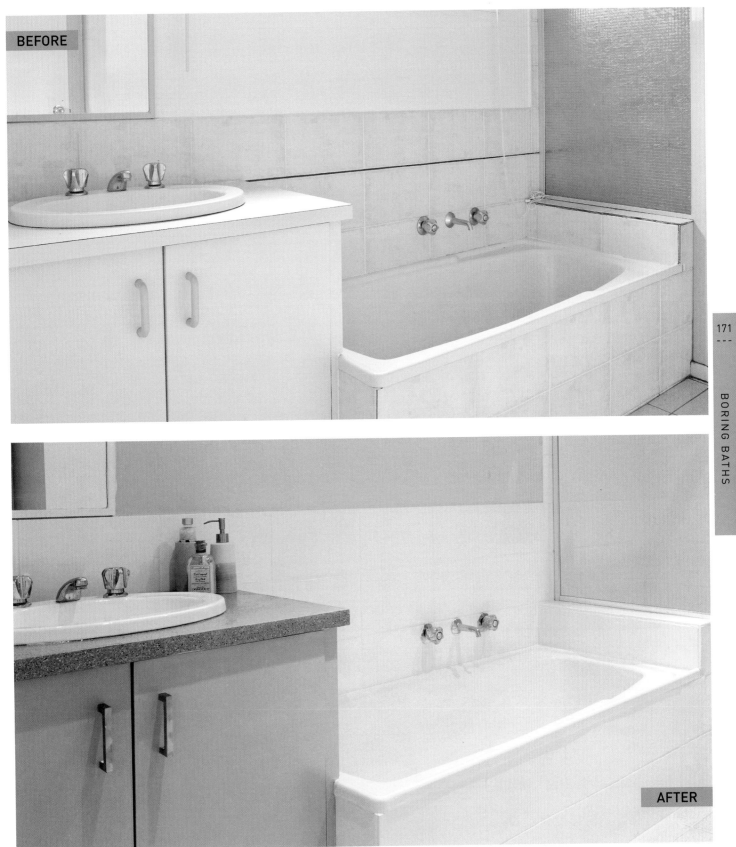

BEFORE

AFTER

THE STRIPTEASE

Maybe your bathroom requires a full-on strip out? The layout may be all wrong, fixtures are past their use-by date and you've decided no amount of specialty paint is going to resurrect your bathroom from the dead.

If a brand spanking new bathroom is on the agenda, you'll be pleased to know there are some great ways to save on costs here, too.

PERFECT PLUMBING

Plumbing labour is one of the biggest costs in any bathroom reno. There are plenty of good plumbers around, with most plumbers charging between $70 and $120 per hour as a general rule of thumb.

One of the most efficient ways to minimise your plumbing bill is to keep all of your plumbing lines on one bathroom wall. It is possible to have the toilet, vanity, shower and bath in a straight line on one wall. This means your plumber is only running water lines in one small section of the room instead of around all of your walls, which cuts your plumbing costs dramatically. See page 179 for a good example of this.

BEFORE

AFTER

This bathroom was super challenging and the space couldn't be increased. It was so small; short in depth and width. It's not perfect by a long shot but I managed to squeeze everything in, including substantial bathroom storage.

WONDERFUL WATERPROOFING

One of your most important jobs when renovating a bathroom is to professionally waterproof all walls and floors before any of your new tiles or fixtures go back in. This is going to cost you $$$.

Waterproofing is a critical component and the foundation of any good bathroom. Put simply, without good protection in place, your bathroom won't last long – water damage is the reason why some bathrooms, without correct waterproofing in place, only last a couple of years at best.

Check out the photo on page 159 – this is a TV reno I did. All of the flooring had completely rotted. When I ripped up the floor tiles, I found that no waterproofing had been installed at all. Some dodgy tradesperson (maybe they weren't even that) had skipped this important step.

Worse still, they had installed a chipboard floor instead of compressed fibro. Shame! At any moment, that floor could have collapsed completely and this home owner was lucky we got involved when we did. Imagine being naked in the shower and your floor collapsing completely? Needless to say, I ripped out the entire flooring and re-installed everything correctly.

Yes, there are DIY waterproofing kits you can pick up from hardware stores, but it's something you should <u>never</u> do yourself. People make the mistake of thinking waterproofing is about slapping some thick compound all over your bathroom floors and walls. Oh, they are so wrong!

There's a skill and technique to the application and you need to allow for expansion and contraction – you need to keep it a certain thickness so it can change once cured. Building standards have minimum quality requirements in this regard. Don't fluff around with this. Get a waterproofing professional in to do your bathroom right. It's going to cost between $600 and $1000, so put that in your budget and don't look back.

There comes a moment when you just have to say goodbye to your tiles and fixtures and send them to bathroom heaven. The pale yellow colour scheme and brown floor tiles make this room look tired and old. And, with no storage, it's simply impractical.

AFTER

Hello, gorgeous! With the freestanding
bathtub, matching wall and floor tiles and
new vanity and toilet, this bathroom now
looks modern, functional and inviting.

BEFORE

Sometimes a bathroom is just too far gone to save. In this case, it could have been salvaged, however the layout was really doing the rest of the newly renovated home a disservice and devaluing the property as a whole.

AFTER

Clean, modern, on-trend … this transformed space ticks all the boxes and looks luxurious. It creates a spa-like atmosphere and in turn lifts the value of the entire property. It's a completely new bathroom, but I saved money by keeping all the plumbing lines on one wall. This layout is also best for small bathrooms.

TILE TRICKS

Tiles make or break your space. The secret is balance in your colour palette. All white can look great with chrome appliances, but tiles are also an opportunity to add a bit of colour. **One important rule**: steer clear of wild, wacky and ultra-colourful patterns – they make your bathroom date too quickly. Also beware of highly polished gloss tiles on the floor – add water and someone is going to crack their head on the bath, guaranteed.

I always go for lighter tiles on my walls and darker tiles on the floor. You don't ever want lighter coloured tiles on your bathroom floor or you'll constantly be looking at dirt, dust and pubic hair. Gross!! You can definitely use coloured tiles, but play it safe and choose two complementary hues. My fail-safe combination is stone-coloured polished tiles for walls and chocolate brown tiles on the floor, with chrome appliances.

Another trick to have up your sleeve is to play with proportions. Going with larger tiles makes a bathroom look bigger than using smaller tiles. It's one of those optical illusions you can use in renovating.

It's also important to know that tiles are <u>not</u> a DIY project. You should never attempt to do it on your own because it's a skill that requires precise work and mistakes cannot be fudged.

TIPS WHEN CHOOSING TILES

Size

One of my favourite tile sizes is 300 mm by 600 mm.

Tile lay and grout lines – modern versus classic

Ensure your tiles are laid horizontally – the lines make the space seem to expand. If you're dreaming of a truly modern look in your new bathroom, always instruct your tiler to lay your wall tiles in what is called the 'stack bond' pattern with end-matched grout lines. In this technique, one tile is stacked directly under the other and all grout lines are in a straight line. Stack bond looks best for bathrooms with an overall modern appearance (and modern adds value). If you want to have a more traditional look, the 'subway' pattern is the way to go. It uses a staggered technique that gives a classic look, but it's not space enhancing and it's not modern. The subway pattern is great for more traditional-looking bathrooms.

Floor

Floor tiles should be end matched as well. A true win is to have the grout lines running from walls to floor. Always do the floors first and then the walls. Always.

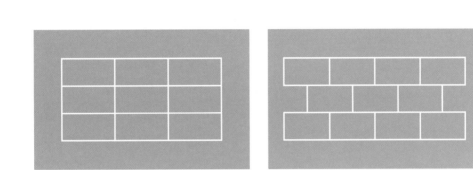

STACK BOND PATTERN   SUBWAY PATTERN

HOT TIP

Tiles come in colour batches
so be sure to order your tiles
in one lot.

SHOWER SCENE

Do you know what I think of first when I think about an old bathroom from the 1970s? That brown-tinted glass with the wire through it. Who the hell thought that was a good idea? But the lesson we can learn from these past horrors is how important colour is in such a small space.

You won't be surprised to hear me say that white and chrome should be your main colour choices for fixtures in your bathroom. Think back to those dorky old shower screens with that solid block of dull colour.

Coloured shower screens visually cut your room in half, making your bathroom look smaller. So the first thing you need to do if your old bathroom has one of those coloured relics is to rip it out and replace it with a clear glass shower screen with a satin chrome trim. Boom! Your bathroom looks double the size.

Remember: Never install a shower screen yourself. Again, it's a specialised task that a licensed shower installer should do. A good experienced handyman or carpenter could also install this for you, but they may take longer to complete the task.

BEFORE

AFTER

This was a one-day reno. Talk about pressure! I rounded everyone up (well there weren't that many of us actually). Tile paint, new shower screen, new blind, new vinyl flooring – it ain't that hard, people!

BEFORE

Wow, this one is wrong on so many levels. The floor tiles are an interesting choice, but so were many other things, back in the 1970s. And what's the go with the out-there, blue storage cabinet? Mirror, mirror on the wall ... who is the bluest of them all? Bonus points for the matching blue toilet seat. This bathroom was also decked out in ... wait for it ... fish border feature tiles!!! Let me pick myself up off the floor, now that I've stopped rolling around in fits of laughter.

AFTER

Can I just say, painting over the fish feature tiles was so incredibly satisfying on this project! I love tile paint; it covers a multitude of sins. The old floor tiles had to stay due to budget constraints but by adding brown paint on the walls, we tied it all together and it looks that bit nicer. The white contrasting tiles in the middle break up the brown. And swapping the coloured shower screen for clear glass makes your bathroom instantly appear larger.
Less disco. Happy days. Project cost: under $1200.

BEFORE

Hey, the 1970s just called – they want their bathroom back! Also, why was everyone hiding behind these brown glass showers back then anyway? What can I say about this bathroom? It looks like Kermit the frog has puked in it. The flowers really add some glam, don't you think?

AFTER

This bathroom was completely transformed for just $2563, all said and done. The owners didn't believe they were in the right house after seeing their newly renovated bathroom! It's light, bright and, best of all, looks NOTHING like the before shot. I bought all the fixtures second hand (except the toilet – don't go there). The feature wall tiles cost me just eight bucks and I tile-painted all the remaining tiles. I only moved the toilet into a new position, and waterproofed and re-laid new floor tiles.

ACCESSORISE ME

One of the biggest problems bathroom renovators face is that, in a small space, so many fixtures are crammed in together.

Back in the day, people separated the bath from the shower, often resulting in a tiny pedestal basin squeezed in somewhere. People didn't seem too fussed on how small or crammed things were. As long as they had everything there and working separately, they were happy. How times have changed.

Today, a big part of any good bathroom design is to ensure the space is functional, practical and also good looking. Nowadays, a lot of people opt for a shower over a bath. Why? Because it significantly increases available floor space, to get other important things in, like your big fat vanity with under-bench storage.

Storage is king. In the old days, it was a pedestal vanity with a small medicine cabinet recessed into your wall. Today's vanities are 450, 600, 900 or 1200 mm wide. Do we just collect more stuff these days?

Don't forget your accessories. Fads come and go. I don't follow them. Call me a rebel. At the moment, black is all the rage but I know these items won't look so great in five years' time. Don't polarise your market. It's chrome, chrome, chrome, baby, all the way.

MY TOP TIPS FOR TOWELS

1. Mount two single towel rails (600 or 900 mm) side by side, as opposed to a double towel rail. In my experience, double towel rail holders tend to sag over time due to the weight of multiple wet, and consequently heavy, towels.

2. Heated towel ladders aren't all they're cracked up to be, unless you get a really good one. With a lot of standard models, only parts of your towel actually get heated. Do you want something consuming electricity all day and night, just to get 5 seconds of pleasure?

3. Your towel rails should be cohesive with all your other bathroom accessories, so make sure you buy them as a family of products.

Accessories

The accessories you choose for your bathroom should always match the style of your bathroom. For a modern do, go sleek and unobtrusive. For traditional bathrooms, go for something a bit more ornate.

Towel holder	600 or 900 mm are standard sizes.
Towel ladder	Non-heated or heated. Don't splurge on this.
Hand towel holder	Simple chrome. Optional but not necessary.
Toothbrush holder	Never. Ditch it! Who wants to stare at other people's toothbrushes?
Toilet roll holder	Simple chrome.
Soap dish – in shower	Opt for an open wire holder. Solid soap trays tend to be nothing more than soap-scum collectors.
Soap dish – in bath	Same as above. Optional but not necessary.
Robe hooks	They're practical and cheap, why not? But they don't add any value.

Mirror magic

Mirrors are so important for increasing the sense of space within your bathroom.

Wherever possible, bigger is better. A floor-to-ceiling mirror not only adds an element of prestige but is highly practical too. Who wants to check themselves out in front of all their other family members?

A mirror directly over your vanity is what's required as a minimum. Try and line your mirror up with something significant like your window architrave, and always have your mirror sitting directly above of your vanity top, not halfway up your wall. See page 191 for a good example of this; see how all my lines are consistent? If you're going to do this, you'll need to order a custom-made mirror from your local glazing shop. It won't be expensive.

Get hooked

Robe hooks ... to be or not to be? Why not, they're cheap! My favourite trick is to put two robe hooks higher up on the back of your bathroom door (for the adults) and two robe hooks lower (for the kids). Parents, you are going to love me for this ... now your children don't have an excuse for leaving their wet towels on the floor. Boom!

BEFORE

Small, pokey and with exposed plumbing pipes ... not exactly the best-selling points for your property. The window overhead is preventing a practical mirror from being installed and there's a big dead zone in the left-hand corner. We don't need to say anything about the floor tiles because they should be self-explanatory. The separate toilet sat in the little room next door.

AFTER

This was a demo and start again job. I knocked out the wall between the bathroom and the separate toilet and brought that useable space into the new layout. A bathroom without a toilet is a renovation cardinal sin, in my eyes. The double vanities add a bit of elegance, and cutting the existing window in half allowed for a mirror that now reflects light around the room.

BEFORE

The yellow tiles in this bathroom were certainly making me feel mellow ... and not in a good way. The lack of windows combined with the boring fixtures and fittings makes this a very dull room.

AFTER

Mellow? More like HELLO! Some simple strategic changes really jazz it up. I knocked out the rear wall tiles only and replaced them with a wood look-a-like tile. I added a simple pendant light for extra lighting and a custom-made vintage railway vanity counter. This bathroom now oozes serious industrial style, on a budget.

BEFORE

There's a whole lotta ugly going on in this bathroom. The pink tub, yellow walls and marble haze tiles are screaming out for a makeover.

AFTER

This bathroom no longer screams ugly, and now sings to the tune of a beautiful melody named storage, storage, storage. You can never have enough. It's got all those classic cosmetic fixes that you now know, for less than $1500. I think it's a big improvement, considering!

CHAPTER FIVE

BEDROOM ANTICS

Your master bedroom is right up there on a buyer's or renter's wish list. It's the king of all bedrooms. However, that's not a legitimate reason to splurge away. Let's face it, bedrooms aren't overly complex. Your goal is to make them functional, but uncomplicated. Once you install your bed, your bedside tables, a dresser and a chair, there won't be much space left. Therefore, good spatial planning is key.

In all of your bedrooms, your objective should be to create a calm, warming space. These rooms are the quiet part of your house, your 'sleeping zone', so colours, your soft furnishings and your styling are of utmost importance in achieving this goal. Avoid bright colours that stimulate, not relax, your senses. You want a peaceful sanctuary to lay your weary head at the end of the day, not a rockstar room that looks and feels like a nightclub.

BEAUTIFUL BEDHEADS

When you're planning the fit-out of any of your bedrooms, one of the first things you need to decide is which wall your bed will go on. It pretty much makes or breaks the entire room and will determine everything, right down to what furniture you put in the room and where each piece sits. Stand in your space and try and visualise where your bed should be, how all your other furniture will work around it and whether the flow feels right. You've got to be able to move freely around your bedroom.

For me, a huge no-no is a bed under a window. In terms of light, it's a bit of a disaster because you'll be up with the birds. Sunlight filtering through your blinds and into your eyes is never fun. And for safety reasons, having your bed (and subsequently your head) right under the window is not the best of sleeping arrangements. Therefore, if possible, always aim to keep your bed against an internal wall without windows.

Once you've determined what wall your bed will be against, you have also, by default, determined your feature wall. Yes, in most cases, the wall behind your bed will be your feature wall so that, visually, your eye gravitates in one direction when you enter the room.

BEFORE

AFTER

A room with a view is a wonderful thing. With that in mind, I opted for a natural colour scheme, treating this room to cosy chocolate hues, without being too heavy. The bedhead statement wall gets some retro-inspired wallpaper and is teamed with lush bedding, with pops of orange. Simplistic bedside lighting, furniture and matching curtains tie it together.

DIY FEATURE WALL

Every bedroom needs a little pick-me-up. Something that stops you in your tracks and makes you say, 'wow, that looks great'. This feature wall is a quick and easy way to add that wow factor to your bedroom, and all within budget.

What you'll need

Three 90 mm wide timber slats, cut to the required size (any sort is OK; see instructions for measurements)
Saw (optional)
Level
1 tube strong construction adhesive
1 tube gap filler
Paint
Paint roller
Paintbrush

Ready, set, go

1. Find and mark out the centre of your wall.

2. Measure the width of your bed and add room to allow for your bedside tables. Your feature wall frame should extend beyond your bedside tables slightly (see the bottom image on the opposite page). This measurement determines the length of your horizontal slat.

3. Mark out where the left and right edges of your frame need to sit on your wall, using your centre wall mark to ensure even spacing.

4. Work out what height you would like your feature frame to be. This determines the length of the vertical slats.

5. Buy your slats, then grab a saw, or have your local hardware store cut the pieces to length for you. Ask them to do a mitre cut in the corners.

6. Grab a tube of strong construction adhesive and glue your timber frame to your wall. Use a level to ensure that the frame does not sit lopsided.

7. Run a bead of gap filler around all edges, then simply paint to any colour of your choice. I like to paint the wall inside the frame a darker colour and the surrounding wall a lighter shade, with the timber slats in between.

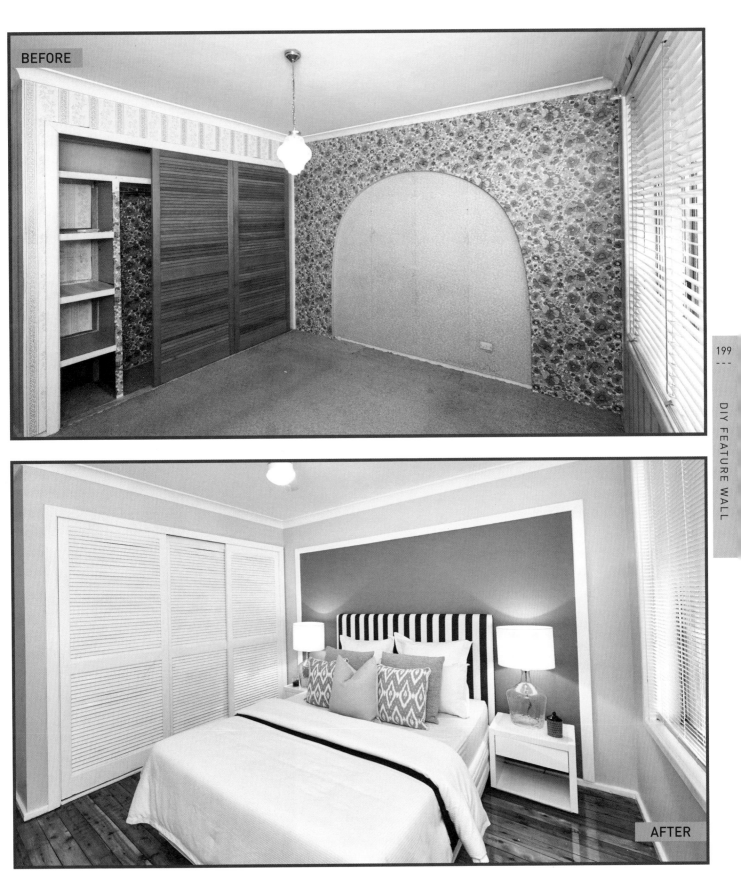

AFTER

BEFORE

When I look at this photo, my eyes don't know what to zoom in on first.
There's a lot going on and not a lot of flow to the room. For a start,
there's two separate beds, pushed together at different angles, with
mismatched bedding. Ugly window furnishings, teamed with the dark
blue walls, aren't making this the perfect colour combo.

AFTER

Coming from the previous hodgepodge of a room, this new bedroom
looks like it has stepped straight out of a magazine feature on a
New York penthouse. With its sleek and sophisticated lines, this
beautiful feature wall pays homage to this lovely space, which I'm
sure most people would be happy to sleep in at night. You can never
go wrong with a classic black-and-white colour scheme. It looks
powerful but not overdone.

BEFORE

This isn't a terrible space. It's your clinical white, but it does have quite a bit of storage, for the size of the room. It needs a little wow-factor to transform this blank and boring space into something special. I'm so happy I don't need to install cupboards, which gives me extra money for decorative items like lighting and shelving.

AFTER

Colour works in bedrooms, and this is a great example of how to do it right. The beautiful wall colour makes it feel inviting and less hospital-like. And check out that new vinyl plank flooring – the walnut colour works so well with the walls. The custom timber shelving above the bedhead draws the eye upwards, making it feel bigger. And my favourite detail is the little desk I've created out of the shelving. So handy and incredibly simple!

BEFORE

This studio apartment had gorgeous exposed rafters but that was the only nice thing in the place. These types of apartments often have everything exposed, so they can feel claustrophobic and as though your life is on full display. As there are no internal walls, they often lack a delineation of zones, resulting in things being placed randomly.

AFTER

Boy oh boy, my thinking cap really did go into overdrive on this one. But, what a spectacular result. I added in walls to create zones. The exposed industrial beams created the backdrop for this truly sexy space. I followed on with a wallpaper in black and gold that mimicked the look of aged pressed metal, which I think is out of this world. I kept the sophisticated black-and-gold colour scheme going with the bedding and throw pillows. This bedroom has glamour written all over it. The home owner loved it, called me a genius even! Now that's going a bit far, but thank you.

LET THERE BE LIGHT

So many bedrooms have a gloomy oyster-style light slapped on the middle of the ceiling. It's the worst. The first favour you should do your master bedroom is to rip out that oyster light. You have a couple of options for the bedroom lighting situation, but they all make a huge difference to the level of comfort and liveability of the room.

Do you know what bedrooms also need more of? A bit of ventilation. You can do far worse than treat yourself to a little free-flowing air. Enter stage left: the ceiling fan. It can do no harm to your room, and you can even grab very affordable ones with a light attached in the middle, killing two decorating birds with one stone. It's only going to cost you about $90.

In the renovation game, you never repeat mistakes. One of my early stuff-ups was installing my downlights too close to my ceiling fan. You've got to be at least 700 mm away from any of the ceiling fan blades, otherwise you get a disco strobing effect at night. Your bedrooms are for sleeping, not clubbing!

Please also be aware that you need to install the wardrobes before your lighting. It changes the dimensions of the space and proportions of the room.

HOW TO ROUGH-IN YOUR DOWNLIGHTS

Once you've got your major elements in place, you can rough-in your downlights. For your average-sized room – say 4 metres by 4 metres – I like to work with the formula of 0.8 to 1.2 metres in from each corner (again, taking into account the wardrobe). Generally, this gives you the best level of lighting for your space.

Another neat little trick is to hang pendant lights on each side of the bedhead, creating a clever alternative to table lamps. Again, work out exactly where the bed will be placed, and work with the main colour of your walls to add that extra dash of style.

BEFORE

A very uninspiring bedroom where the bed looks too big for the space.
I see this kind of look all the time: white walls, vertical drapes and
oversized furniture. It's a classic look, especially in a lot of older-style
apartments. You don't need to be a design genius to work it out; there's
not a lot going on and it's definitely not the type of room you would ever
get excited about.

AFTER

I only had $5000 to renovate the whole apartment, so I kept the bedroom
simple but I think I achieved my goal of making it look better than
before. By using the window as a bedhead (which I normally wouldn't
do), I've created a sense of space, with more free-flowing access to the
wardrobe. The window furnishings, floor covering, bedside lighting
and neutral tones have now given this previously tired bedroom a fresh,
modern and inviting feel.

THE ART OF STORAGE

There's a very sexy word you can use in the bedroom to spice things up ... storage. A clever, fuss-free and simple way to declutter a space and preserve sanity will always be worth a million bucks in the bedroom. But, like all my advice, it doesn't have to cost the earth. A simple flat-pack solution can be purchased from most major hardware stores and can be self assembled. Please remember to bolt your wardrobe cabinetry to your walls for added safety.

I don't think you can go past the tried and tested brilliance of a simple mirrored wardrobe. It's economical, bounces light around the space, enhances the feeling of spaciousness and has a timeless look. And who knows, it could add a little va-va-voom to your night life, too ... wink, wink.

BEFORE

AFTER

The best thing about storage?
It hides all your stuff from prying
eyes, and nothing clutters your
space! Plus, mirrored wardrobes
are highly practical, and what girl
(and guy) doesn't love that?

BEFORE

This bedroom is a great example of not making the most of your proportions. Moving around this space is just going to get annoying, and that's the last thing you should feel in a bedroom. The current storage and colour scheme is mismatched and just looks old. I needed to give it all a boot into the 21st century.

AFTER

A new mirrored wardrobe and feature wall give this bedroom some breathing space. The wardrobe stashes away all those bits and pieces that visually clutter a space. I also love that the wardrobe's mirrored doors reflect the window opposite. I kept things grounded with new timber laminate flooring and my favourite wallpaper made its star appearance again in this property. A simple, stainless steel ceiling fan and light combo add air movement and much-needed light.

BEFORE

When I saw this three-bedroom house, my mind started ticking over with all the possibilities. From all my years of renovating, I know that certain rooms sometimes end up as a dead zone, sitting there serving no real purpose. Sometimes it can be beneficial, both financially and functionally, to rejig part of the layout.

AFTER

And this was the result. I added a timber stud wall (in the section where the arch is) and created a whole new bedroom, taking it from a three- to four-bedroom house, at a minimum cost. Boom, up goes my property value! It was a practical move because who needs an L-shaped lounge room, anyway? Plus, this house had a second living area in another part of the house.

I bought this property for $550,000, spent $67,500 on the reno and had it revalued 15 days later for $690,000. In the space of three weeks, I manufactured instant equity that meant I could go to the bank and do it all again.

FLOOR SHOW

What lies beneath makes up a substantial part of your room's look and feel. Personally, I like flooring to be uniform across the entire house. So if you go for floorboards (or tiles) in your living zone, then use these in the bedrooms too.

Carpet requires a bit more attention and easily gets trashed if subjected to the whims of renters. It needs regular maintenance and care to last the distance. Having said all that, there are certain buyers who prefer carpet, so keep the end game in mind and do your research into your area before you get the flooring in place.

The same goes for tiles. In hotter climates and beachside residences, tiles can be a pretty easy solution.

BEFORE

This tired old bedroom needs a complete makeover. The carpet is old and bland, the wall colour is boring and the window furnishings need some imagination. And who wants the neighbours looking in all the time anyway?

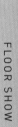

AFTER

I started from the ground up and made everything new again. It doesn't even look like the same room. New lighting, window furnishings, wall colour, ceiling fan and, most importantly, new flooring give this bedroom more depth, sophistication and appeal.

BEFORE

There is nothing especially wrong with this bedroom, except its outdated decor. Twenty years ago, the peach-coloured carpet and matching scalloped drapes would have been all the rage. This master bedroom is a great size and is just screaming out for a bit of modernising. I had to tie the whole look in to the rest of the house that I was renovating.

AFTER

And I was right. The home owner wanted carpet to stay in the bedrooms so I simply installed new carpet, in a different colour and texture. An on-trend colour scheme and painted feature wall, teamed with contrasting curtains, provide much-needed depth to the room. The lush bed linen ties all the colours in the room, and gorgeous styling transforms the bedroom into a heavenly space, with a touch of elegance. All on a budget, of course!

BEFORE

Why do so many people have boring bedrooms? It doesn't need to be this way! I personally wouldn't want to sleep in this room. The walls need a freshen up, along with the carpet and window furnishings.

AFTER

What a difference snazzy new timber laminate flooring, a tin of paint and furnishings can make. This bedroom looks sleek and modern with its neutral tones. I added a simple but visually striking wall-hung bio-ethanol heater that adds a point of difference. I think there will be some serious romance going on ...

COLOUR ME HAPPY

Now, the bedroom is a place where you can go a little wild ... with colour. But not too wild. Nothing kinky, please – you don't want to feel slightly ill or unsettled. There has been some fascinating research into the effect of colour on mood and it turns out that vibrant yellows in big doses can actually make people feel anxious, so I suggest leaving out the yellows and opting instead for soft, calming hues and tones like blue-greys, beiges and stone colours. Your room feels all the more enveloping and cosy with a dash of these in the mix. Try to stay away from simple white. In the bedroom, it often comes across as cold and clinical and you need to add that all-important sense of luxury and comfort. So colour is critical.

I've even gone very dark and handsome for one of my projects and the result is actually quite polarising (see opposite). It worked for the project and the buyers but, for broader appeal, go soft rather than heavy.

BEFORE

BEFORE

This neat and tidy space is the sort of blank canvas that I love. It can easily be transformed into a stylish bedroom at a very small cost. And keeping the costs down is what we all love.

AFTER

With a paintbrush in hand, I've transformed the space that previously looked like a tap-dancing studio. I then added new curtains and neutral styling with a splash of colour. It's a fresh, modern bedroom without all the pomp and pageantry.

BEFORE

Doesn't this look like a bedroom we've all seen before? The striped duvet cover, timber bedhead and furniture. There are bits and pieces everywhere. No doubt a bit of love and kindness will transform this bedroom into a masterpiece.

AFTER

Voila! I had just six hours to transform this little ugly duckling into a beautiful swan. It was a one-day TV challenge on a budget, with the standout being the crisscross timber feature wall, which gives the large space behind the bed an interesting twist. The new dark curtains add a block-out feature, which will help with weekend sleep-ins, and the new timber laminate floorboards give the bedroom a much fresher look compared to the old concrete floor.

AFTER

How much better does this entire room look, just from the choice of paint colours? The simple tonal switch has given the room much-needed depth. The window furnishings add both convenience and elegance, with the slimline venetians paired with brown velvet blockout drapes from Ikea.

BEFORE

This empty, boring bedroom gave me the chance to let my imagination run wild – and who doesn't love an opportunity like this?

AFTER

You should never ignore your room's best features, and in this case a double-sized window becomes the star attraction, thanks to the floor-to-ceiling drapes. Added sheers offer day-long privacy without losing sunlight. There's a striking contrast in light and dark colours in this room but it all blends in beautifully.

KIDS' ROOMS

Now you can have a bit of fun with these rooms, but keep it flexible. Too many people make the overall 'blue or pink' mistake. Don't pick a team; go gender-neutral instead, with any unisex tone you like. Then add a fun colour with the bedding. Again, you can make up a feature wall for the kids – I am a big fan of decals because you get the same effect as wallpaper without the hassle or the commitment, and we all know about the fickle nature of kids' trends.

Storage is your number-one priority here, but again, I must emphasise the importance of making absolutely sure that everything is secured to the wall, because kids will climb given the opportunity. You have to think like a kid. You do not want anything to fall on top of a child. Aside from it being truly awful, you also have a responsibility to ensure the house you create is safe, and, in the worst-case scenario, you can also be financially liable for a terrible accident. So let's avoid all that unpleasantness by making sure everything is safe and secure.

This also goes for blinds. The cord can be a choking hazard and so I recommend mounting the cords higher up on your window architrave, so it's not as easily reached and it doesn't become a noose.

BEFORE

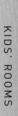

AFTER

I'm a mum and let me tell you, my daughter would not have been excited to play in this room as it was before. Now, the off-white paint on the walls, dressed with colourful accessories, makes it easy to update this room as your child grows.

BEFORE

How ugly is this room? Imagine coming home to this every night.
It looks like someone has been murdered here. It's your classic
cosmetic renovation, working largely with something that has good
bones. I'm not sure what happened to the wallpaper. Maybe someone
started removing it but lost interest? The ceiling pendant should be
in a museum, and the lack of anything in this room makes it the sort
of property I get excited about. For me, the uglier, the better!

AFTER

The rest of the wallpaper was removed by rollering hot soapy water
directly onto the walls (just use a mild detergent in your hot water).
I let that sit for an hour, then I scraped it all off. On went the new paint,
with contrasting window trims and skirting boards. A simple venetian
covers an ugly window, but, looking back now, I should have installed
curtains as well. Surprisingly, there were gorgeous floorboards under
the ramshackle flooring, which were brought back to life with the
help of my floor sander. The walls and floor coverings made the
biggest difference, proving that anything and everything is possible
on a small budget.

ADDED EXTRAS

You've heard the saying 'under-promise, over-deliver'. Well, that's exactly what I did in this master bedroom.

Sometimes you just want to lie in bed and watch TV. But who wants a chunky TV cabinet in their bedroom? I created this non-structural feature wall in front of my wardrobes. It is about 1.8 metres in width and features a flat-screen TV mounted on the front. This means it consumes only minimal floor space, which is perfect. But the back of this wall is the true star. It contains ten long shelves that neatly house up to 40 pairs of shoes. Ladies – heaven! In this instance, I created something out of nothing and it wasn't wildly expensive.

There are a lot of little extras you can add to your bedroom – you just have to put your thinking cap on and work out whether that change is worth the investment. Could you get some floor to ceiling glass on one part of your bedroom wall so you've got a real practical mirror to get dressed in front of each morning?

Shelving, little reading nooks in rooms that have bay windows ... the options are endless. Just remember, don't go too crazy in this room, spending your hard-earned cash.

ENSUITE DREAMS

In an ideal world, your master bedroom would have an ensuite. But it's not always essential. If you have three bedrooms or less, you can get away without one. The game usually changes when you have four bedrooms or more – it creates buyer expectations for second bathrooms or ensuites. Saying that, if your property is of lower value, a single bathroom alone can be sufficient. There are lots of variables and rules in property, so do your research.

What you may not realise is that even though ensuites are small, they're going to cost you almost as much as a full-sized bathroom. They're not cheap rooms to install due to all the services, fixtures and fittings required, so think long and hard if the spend is warranted. Ask local real estate agents if they think it's overkill. And keep in mind, a dated old ensuite doesn't always need to be demolished. Sometimes small cosmetic tweaks are all that's needed.

ABOUT THE AUTHOR

Cherie Barber is Australia's renovation queen, one of the stars of Network 10's *The Living Room* and a regular TV renovator on Network 9's *Today Extra Show* and *Sky News Business*. Cherie is also a weekly radio presenter, highly sought-after public speaker, author, award-winning business woman and the host of US TV show *5 Day Flip*.

At the age of 21, Cherie embarked on a minor renovation and cosmetically flipped her first property, making a profit in the process, which sparked her interest in property. She bought another unrenovated house straight after and the rest, as they say, is history. Twenty-seven years later, she's now personally renovated over 100 properties (and counting).

In 2009, Cherie established her company, Renovating For Profit, after constantly being asked about how she did what she did.

She mentors Australia's largest community of renovators and with more than 11,000 Aussies having undergone her training, Cherie is the market leader for quality property renovation education. This, combined with her extensive media presence, makes her Australia's leading media authority on anything relating to property renovation. She is considered by many to be renovation royalty, both in Australia and internationally.

In addition to her significant renovation achievements, Cherie has been a finalist twice in the Telstra Business Woman of the Year Awards and in 2016, was named as one of the Top 100 Women of Influence in Australia. She is a national brand ambassador for Asbestos Awareness and is passionate about educating home owners and DIYers on how to renovate safely when asbestos is present. She lists her most significant role as being a mother to her 11-year-old daughter, Milan.

ACKNOWLEDGEMENTS

You can't be a successful renovator as a one-woman band. I am truly blessed to have incredible people around me and there are so many people to thank. This is your book as much as it is mine.

The media – to Network 7, Network 9, 9Life, *The Today Extra Show*, Foxtel, *Sky News Business*, and especially to Network Ten/WTFN Productions for having me on your show, *The Living Room* for the last six years. Without your support, it would be impossible to pass on my renovation knowledge to help others. A special thanks to HGTV in America for having me host *5 Day Flip*. What an experience! To the press, thank you for all the interviews over the years and for never twisting things around to make me sound bad. And to Macquarie Media, for having me on your radio show each week.

Hardie Grant Publishing – to the wonderful team at Hardie Grant. Thank you for being such a nice bunch of people to work with, and for bringing this book to fruition.

My representatives – to Melita from One Management (my talent agent) who said I should do a book or two or three. Number one is now done! To Polkadot PR, your fun now begins. Please try and sell more than five copies.

My students – there are over 11,000 of you out there and I wish I knew you all personally. I love all of you for the people that you already are, and the people that you want to be. I am truly humbled that you call me your mentor and look to me for guidance. You are my inspiration ...

My RFP team – to my wonderful team at RFP headquarters (all 20 of you) who run my office and public speaking business. Within the walls of RFP headquarters, my nickname is "The Tsunami". I make an appearance every 3 months, flying into the office unannounced, putting everyone in a spin, then flying out again. I drive you all insane, but I know that you all secretly love it!

I love you all. You are all the women and men behind the woman. I couldn't do it without you. My heartfelt gratitude to all of you.

My tradespeople and suppliers, past and present – I have worked with some truly amazing tradespeople over the last 27 years and a few dodgy ones too. To the questionable ones, thank you for helping me make mistakes. I have learnt something from all of you. To all my amazing tradies, past and present – I could not have done this without you. Thank you for all the laughs over the years and for helping me beautify Australia, one ugly house at a time. A special thanks to my current two main men, Paul my carpenter and my 2IC, Mickey The Chippy. Simply the best!

My Family – to Mum for being a great mum, always having a go and staying happy, no matter what. To Dad, for instilling in me great morals and a good work ethic from such a young age. There is no free path to wealth. To my brothers Rodney, Mick and Greg – thank you for being great brothers. To all my little sisters Jeneane, Susie and Kylie – I may earn more money than you, but that is not an excuse to keep stealing my clothes! To Steve – we are no longer together, but you will always be my family, until the day I pop my clogs. Thank you for helping me with Milan on late night TV renos.

My partner, Matt – thank you for always being there for me in every way. They say third time lucky ... And for the record everyone – he has never been a renovator, nor will he be!

Last but not least – **my daughter, Milan** – you are my everything, my biggest achievement, by far. Everything I do is for you. However, if you could find it in your heart to stop charging me $10 for every trip that we make to the hardware store after school pick-up, mummy would really love that. And if you ever decide not to become a fashion designer, and you want to be a renovator instead, I will have a pair of workboots waiting for you. Blinged up, of course!

Published in 2018 by Hardie Grant Books, an imprint of Hardie Grant Publishing

Hardie Grant Books (Melbourne)
Building 1, 658 Church Street
Richmond, Victoria 3121

Hardie Grant Books (London)
5th & 6th Floors
52–54 Southwark Street
London SE1 1UN

hardiegrantbooks.com

A Cataloguing-in-Publication entry is available from the catalogue of the National Library of Australia at www.nla.gov.au

Renovating For Profit
ISBN 978 1 74379 407 4

Publishing Director: Pam Brewster
Managing Editor: Marg Bowman
Project Editor: Anna Collett
Editor: Anna Collett
Editorial Assistant: Serena Thompson
Proofreader: Allison Hiew
Design Manager: Jessica Lowe
Internal design and layout: Sinéad Murphy
Cover design: Vaughan Mossop
Photographers: Richard Mortimer, Kate Nutt
Production Manager: Todd Rechner, Tessa Spring

Colour reproduction by Splitting Image Colour Studio

Printed in China by 1010 Printing International Limited